Offshore Development and Technical Support

Proven Strategies and Tactics for Success

M. M. Sathyanarayan

GlobalDev Publishing • Cupertino, CA

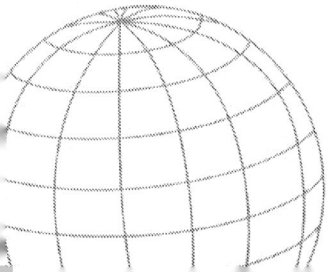

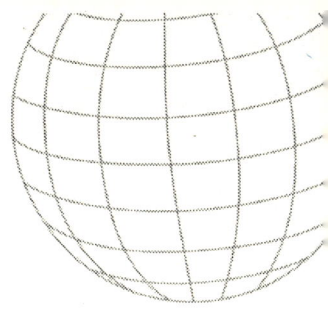

Offshore Development

and Technical Support

by

M. M. Sathyanarayan

Contents

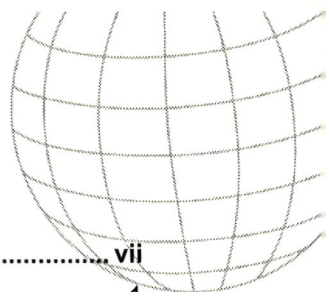

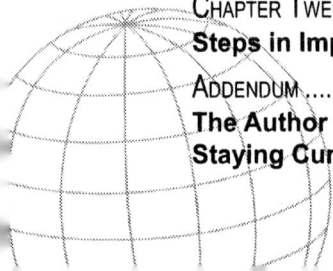

Acknowledgments

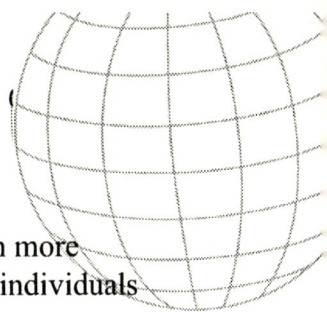

In completing this book, I have received assistance from more people than I can name. I acknowledge and thank these individuals who generously contributed energy and time.

Avron Barr

Bonnie Boyce

Scott Brown

V. Chandrasekaran

Dave Cutler

Coby Dunn

Don Fowler

Audrey Fricke

John Houghton

Don Huntington

Sridhar Mitta

Watson Murthy

Rishi Navani

Alan Rush

Kripa Sathyanarayan

Ramesh Sekar

Dan Shafer

J. Sriram

Shirley Tessler

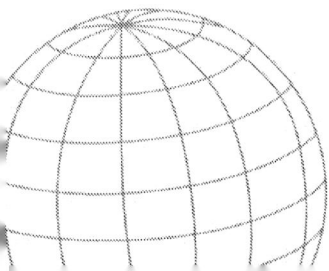

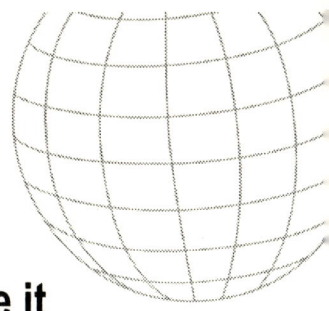

CHAPTER ONE

What this book is and how to use it

You will find this book useful in the following ways:

If you are...	Then this book will...
...responsible for software development, technical support, internal IT, call center/help desk, professional services or business process outsourcing, and a beginner in leveraging offshore resources	...help you reach your business objectives more rapidly with a higher level of confidence
...already engaged in offshore development	...provide ideas for improving your operations
...an offshore vendor	...provide insights into your customers' decision making

In addition, the book provides guidelines for dealing with these frequently asked questions:

- ◆ Why consider offshore development?
- ◆ Is offshore development right for you?
- ◆ What types of projects qualify for offshore development?
- ◆ What are the hidden costs of offshoring?
- ◆ Do you set up your own operation or outsource?
- ◆ How do you select the best potential partner?
- ◆ What is the best way to organize for success?
- ◆ How do you integrate your operation with the offshore operation — not just the engineering processes, but the management processes?
- ◆ How do you gain visibility, control projects remotely and measure results?
- ◆ How do you manage risks?
- ◆ How do you gain lasting competitive advantage from offshoring?

"Development" is used in a general sense throughout this book. It covers all aspects of the software development life cycle — design, development, quality assurance, deployment and technical support. It assumes that you are familiar with the software development process. Certain aspects of technical support require a different approach to implementation and these are presented in a separate chapter.

While the book focuses on software product development and technical support, the best practices presented here also apply to:

♦ Information Systems,
♦ Customer Support,
♦ Call Centers, and
♦ Business Process Outsourcing (BPO).

You can use this book as a guide for:

♦ Management teams preparing strategy and road map for offshore development at the organization and unit levels.

♦ Individual managers and management teams in their ongoing management of offshore development.

With the information provided in this book, you can increase your knowledge of practical, proven best practices in offshore development and technical support.

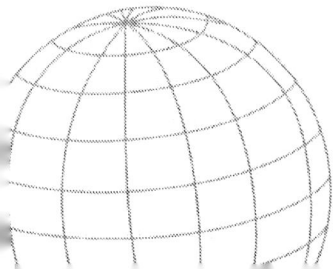

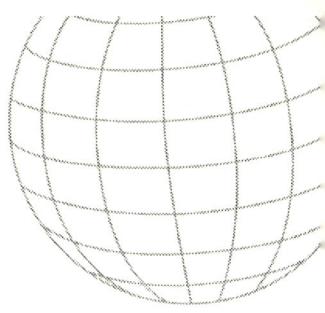

CHAPTER TWO

Overview

In this chapter we address these key questions:

- Why consider offshore development?
- Which countries should you consider?
- What types of projects qualify for offshore development?
- What are the challenges?
- What does it take to succeed?

Why consider offshore development?

The manufacturing sector in the U.S. began leveraging offshore resources decades ago. A similar phenomenon has begun to occur in software development.

Consider the following two points:

- Countries outside the U.S., such as India, China, Russia, and Ireland have large talent pools and these offshore talent pools are expanding at a rapid pace. For example, India produces 350,000 engineers and China produces 600,000 engineers a year, 200,000 of whom are electrical engineers. By contrast, the U.S. produces a mere 70,000 undergraduate and 30,000 graduate engineers.

- Salary levels offshore are a fraction of U.S. salary levels. After taking into account the other costs associated with offshore development, companies can reduce their development expenses by 30% to 50%.

Offshore manufacturing is admittedly simpler than offshore development, since software development is more complex than manufacturing.

Despite the complexities offshore development approach has been proven many times. Since the early 90s a large number of companies have set up offshore development facilities. In addition to Fortune 500 companies, mid-sized companies and startups are leveraging offshore resources. Many venture capitalists now encourage offshoring as part of the strategy for startups. Some have set up operations directly, while others are partnering with local companies.

Here is a sampling of the companies that are utilizing offshore resources either directly through their own operations and/or through local partnerships:

American Express	Hughes Networks	Oracle
British Airways	IBM	Riverstone Networks
Cadence	Intel	Santerra Systems
Cisco	Kanisa	Sun Microsystems
Force Computers	Microsoft	Texas Instruments
GE	Motorola	Tibco
HP	Nortel	Xerox

Note that this list probably includes unfamiliar names, since companies of various sizes and name recognition levels are pursuing offshore development.

However, many companies launch into offshoring without fully understanding the issues and risks. Consequently, many have failed or been only marginally successful. Although the benefits of offshoring are conceptually easy to understand, actual execution is fraught with significant risks. If you learn and adopt practices developed and proven over time by successful companies you will minimize risks and the substantial payback will flow directly to your bottom line.

Let's look at the rewards first, because they can be considerable. A company can use offshore development to:

- ◆ Reduce cost and increase shareholder value
- ◆ Decrease development cycle time and improve customer satisfaction
- ◆ Increase revenues through more development
- ◆ Gain staffing flexibility
- ◆ Meet local requirements
- ◆ Localize products
- ◆ Gain an option to compete against upstarts

Here are the details concerning each.

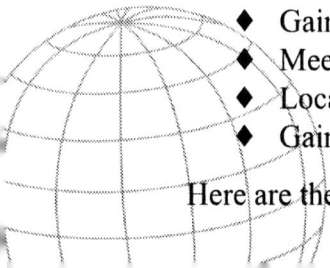

Reduce cost and increase shareholder value

Even after accounting for overhead related to travel, communication infrastructure, and additional bandwidth needed to manage overseas efforts, utilizing offshore talent, when managed effectively, can save 30% to 50% compared with U.S. costs.

This cost reduction gives companies options they may not have had without going offshore. Depending on the needs of the company, savings can either flow to the bottom line or fund other projects or products. In the former case, cost reductions can increase the company's earnings per share (EPS) and thus increase the company's value. In the latter case, the reductions indirectly generate additional revenues and greater profits.

Decrease cycle time and improve customer satisfaction

Developing and supporting software from locations at opposite ends of the world provides an effective method of shortening timelines. When one team is done for the day, the other one is getting started. This provides the ability for around the clock development, QA, and support.

Shortening timelines in this way enables faster development cycles. In any business, time is money. Furthermore, quicker bug fixes increase customer satisfaction at reduced cost while taking advantage of lower labor costs offshore.

Increase revenues through increased development

Demands for new products and new features generally exceed most development budgets. Sometimes useful features are cut because they are not cost-effective or might compromise a release date. However, features that can be developed at reduced time and cost can fit into the product plan.

Gain staffing flexibility

A company doing offshore development can maintain a certain core staff at their headquarters, and if they work with a partner, they can balance staffing requirements, since the value proposition of many such companies is to provide rapid ramp-up and project based staffing.

Short duration projects can be staffed rapidly. It is possible to find a "ready" set of resources including people and necessary infrastructure such as space and standard equipment.

Furthermore, reduced costs for overseas development means that a company on a fixed budget can deploy a larger staff for faster time to market.

Meet local requirements

Some countries have a requirement that companies who sell into their country must also invest in their country. Offshore development provides the ability to satisfy such a requirement.

Localize products

Countries doing offshore development have a greater availability of talent with local language skills supplementing their technical skills.

Gain an option to compete against upstarts

As a company grows, the level of effort required to sustain products also grows. By one estimate as much as 70% of companies' engineering budgets are devoted to sustaining products and feature enhancements.

Allocation of resources into such after-market activities can leave a company at a competitive disadvantage against a startup, which focuses 100% of its budget on new product development. Of course no company can avoid sustaining, but to the degree a company can move this offshore, to that extent it will be able to focus more attention on new products.

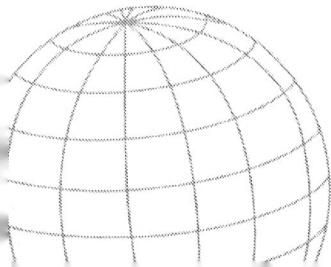

Which countries should you consider?

Several countries provide software development services. The main ones include:

- India
- Ireland
- China
- Russia

India has become the largest player in the field of offshore development for a number of reasons:

- The availability of a very large engineering talent pool.
- An education system that continues to produce large numbers of engineers.
- Widespread knowledge of English language.
- Promotion by the government.
- A western (British) style judicial system.
- Laws protecting intellectual property.

In addition, the Indian software industry has continued to improve its software development processes. It's been estimated that 20 Indian companies have been assessed at CMM Level 5 (which is the highest level one can attain in software process maturity) and some companies are pursuing initiatives like Six Sigma (which was pioneered by GE).

Motorola's development facility in Bangalore was one of the early companies to achieve CMM Level 5 distinction. Many companies with 100-200 employees have achieved CMM Level 3 certification.

Ireland enjoys a location advantage because of its proximity to the European market. Its location combined with the fact that it is an English-speaking country has propelled Ireland to the position of second-largest exporter of software services, after India.

China and Russia have a large base of high quality talent, but the language barrier has limited the type of projects that can be executed from either country.

However, China continues to make a major push in offshore software development to match its burgeoning manufacturing industry. Given its vast talent pool and its focus on this sector, China is likely to become a major force.

What types of projects qualify for offshore development?

During the early 90s, projects considered for offshore development were limited to software maintenance and QA. However, over the course of time, the types of projects has continued to expand. At this time, all the following types of projects are being executed from one or more of the leading countries discussed in the preceding section:

1. **Development**
   - New development
   - Enhancements
   - Sustaining

2. **Quality Assurance and Testing**
   - Development of test suites
   - Test execution for releases
   - Enhancement of test suites
   - Interoperability testing
   - Test automation
   - Test scripting

3. **Support**
   - Technical support
   - Customer support
   - Help desk

4. **Information Systems**
   - Application development and maintenance
   - Network management
   - Web enabling legacy systems

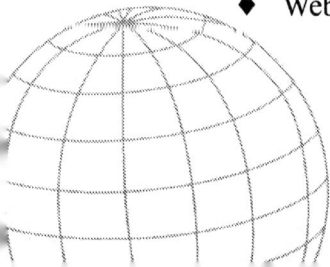

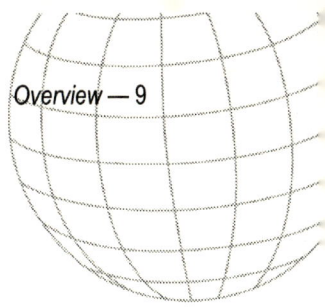

5. Business Process Outsourcing

- ◆ Call centers
- ◆ Payroll services
- ◆ Claims processing
- ◆ Billing services
- ◆ Medical transcription
- ◆ HR applications
- ◆ Telemarketing
- ◆ Order entry

While startups, in general, wish to locate the entire team in one place (at the headquarters), at least one company has located their entire development team offshore.

FROM THE TRENCHES

The U.S. operation features a relatively small staff consisting primarily of customer facing functions. This company is managed by a team of professionals who are well-versed in offshore development.

What are the challenges?

Some companies sign a contract with an overseas vendor and then expect simply to realize the promised advantages. However, to leverage offshore resources successfully, it is essential to put in place a set of management disciplines. The following excerpt from a McKinsey report sums up this point:

> "Without disciplines in managing offshore, a company can not only squander the cost and time savings it had hoped to gain through them but can also face other problems — late deliverables, escalating costs, mismatches between expectations and deliverables, and even outright failure."

> Inigo Amoribieta, Kaushik Bhaumik, Kishore Kanakamedala, and Ajay D. Parkhe.
> *The McKinsey Quarterly,* 2001 No 2

Key challenges include

- Identifying country entry strategies — plus variations in culture, legal systems, and infrastructure.
- Implementing the organizational and operational changes that need to occur at the U.S. headquarters. This key component for achieving success is often overlooked.
- Dealing with impact of distance and time zones.
- Gaining visibility and control of remote development.
- Providing for technology transfers.
- Addressing security and business continuity issues. Subsequent to September 11 this issue has caused significant concern. Processes must be established to ensure effective management of these risks for the long term.

By studying the industry we have ascertained the factors and practices that help companies address these topics and ensure success of their efforts. The next section presents the results of this research.

What does it take to succeed?

What are the key ingredients of a successful offshore development experience? To answer this question, we approached senior executives of multinational companies engaged in this activity to find out what is important, what works, and what doesn't. We conducted competency interviews in which participants were asked to describe both the nature and effectiveness of their offshore programs.

In addition to this research, we drew heavily on our own management experiences in offshore development — both with a large computer company and with our own clients. From these experiences, we identified the major factors that appear to distinguish effective from ineffective offshore development.

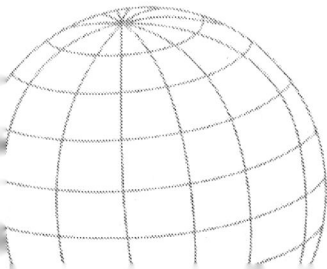

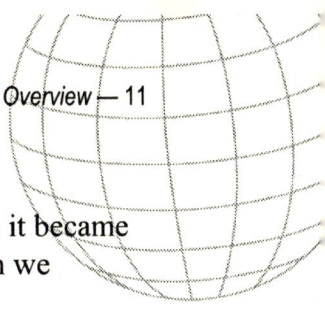

Organization and use of this information

When we began organizing the findings of our research, it became clear that there is a distinct hierarchy of practices, which we designated as "Factors."

Each factor describes a distinction in orientation, attitude, behavior, or business activity that discriminates between effective and ineffective offshore development.

Each best practice contains a similar distinction. Some factors and best practices overlap. They intertwine and are not always clearly separable. Wherever possible, examples are provided to illustrate how someone has applied these best practices. These are under the heading: "From the trenches."

The combined factors and best practices show what discriminates effective from ineffective activity, but do not in any way attempt to describe completely all that is necessary to carry out offshore development.

In this sense, the factors and best practices do not represent a complete "how to" description, but rather they denote items that might improve the chance of success.

Applying the best practices depends on circumstances and upon the use of good management judgment. However, for simplicity we present them as unqualified recommendations.

When applied in combination, the best practices will create a synergistic environment to assure offshore development excellence.

The factors

The following provides a diagrammatic view of the factors. Although there are dependencies, implementation will not be sequential. Synergistic application of these factors will improve cost structure, reduce cycle time, and enhance market share — all of which increase shareholder value.

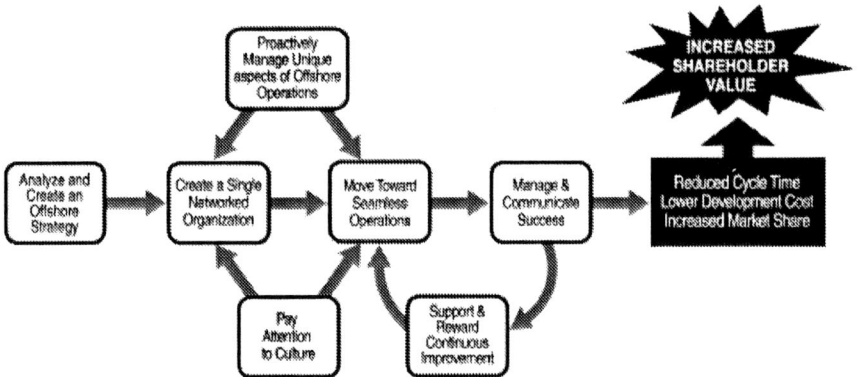

Strategy	Analyze the operation and create an offshore development strategy that fits with your company's business strategy. In order to realize the full benefits, offshore development should be considered a significant strategic initiative that will have an impact on the organization as a whole. Answer the question "Is offshore development right for your situation?" and, if so, put in place the appropriate offshore strategy.
Organization	Rather than create offshore silos, establish one integrated organization. This is true whether you set up your own offshore operation or decide to work with an offshore partner.
Operations	Link the various parts of the operations, so that they operate as one seamless organization despite their geographic separation.

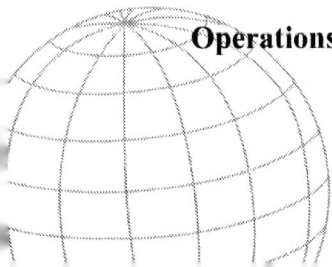

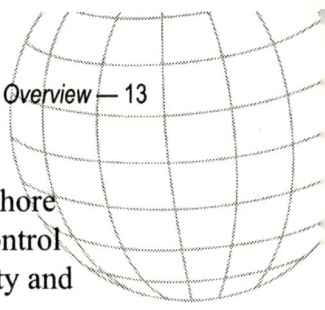

Proactively manage unique aspects of offshore operations
It is essential to proactively establish management disciplines unique to offshore operations. This ranges from export control compliance to mechanisms for visibility and control of remote operations.

Culture
Pay attention to differences in culture. By definition, the organization is entering a different country and hence a different culture and must, therefore, be proactive in establishing policies to deal with cultural differences.

Manage and communicate successes
Carefully orchestrate the initial projects so that they are outstandingly successful and be sure to communicate that to the organization. The success of the initial projects becomes a form of soft selling so that, over a period of time, offshore development gets accepted as a way of life.

Continuous improvement
Practice continuous improvement in all facets of the organization, including offshore development. As managers become comfortable with the approach, they can continue to derive advantages above and beyond cost savings — which is where most companies begin.

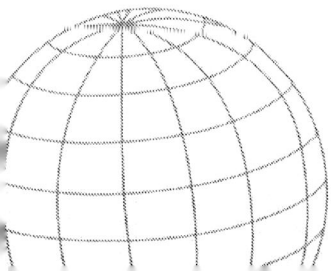

CHAPTER THREE

Analyze and Create an Offshore Strategy

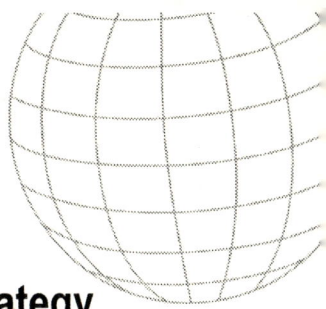

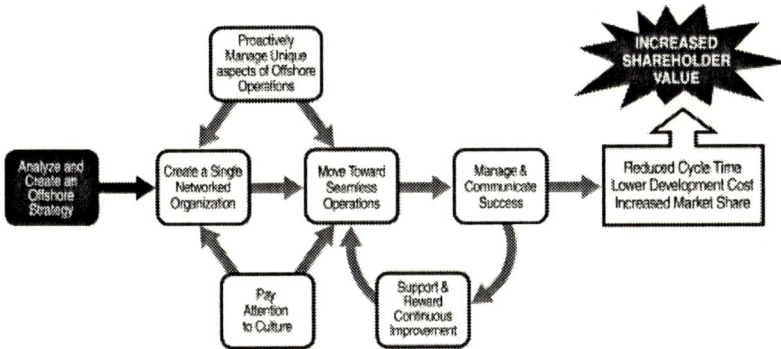

Is offshore development the right strategy for your company? The current trend for leveraging offshore resources does not mean that offshore development is necessarily the right choice for every company. Any process for deciding whether to go offshore or not should include the following key considerations:

♦ Your company's business strategy.
How offshore development can support it.
♦ Size of effort.
The approach to offshore development will vary widely if you are considering a 10-person group offshore versus a 100-person group.
♦ Functions and potential candidate projects.
Identify clear project selection criteria for projects going offshore specific to the company and apply these criteria to identifying candidate projects.
♦ Offshore development expertise, bandwidth, and contacts.
If these are not available inside the company, management must be able to identify and leverage external resources.

15

- Investment and returns.
  Offshore development can generate savings, but during the initial stages the company will have to invest time and money.
- Commitment from top level management.
  Without top level commitment, the company decreases the chances of success in offshore development.
- Organizational readiness

Taking time to decide if offshore development is right is an essential first step for a successful offshore development program. However, it is not uncommon to find companies rushing to negotiate with an offshore vendor to take on a project without giving thought to the long-term viability of the program. This kind of rush into activity rarely works and more often than not is a formula for certain failure.

Best practices

- Define specific business objectives
- Establish project selection criteria
- Determine the form of organization
- Select country for the best long term fit
- Determine entire cost, not just salaries
- Establish major milestones
- Develop a multi-year financial analysis
- Select a strategy to gain momentum

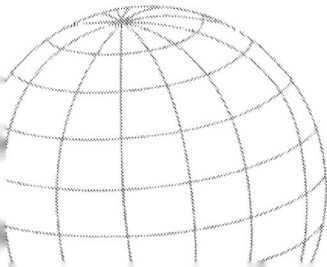

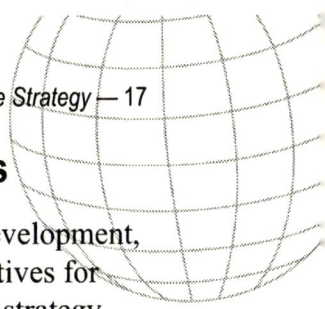

Define specific business objectives

As they approach the challenges of offshore software development, companies must plan to develop specific business objectives for the offshore program that will support overall corporate strategy and objectives. As covered earlier, typical objectives include:

- ◆ Reduce costs
- ◆ Decrease development cycle time
- ◆ Increase revenues through more development
- ◆ Gain staffing flexibility

Many companies ask themselves, "How do we outsource our development offshore to reduce costs?" It's not uncommon for some of these companies to expect overseas costs to be a small fraction of U.S. costs. They focus on salary differentials and tend to underestimate other costs. After trying this approach for a period of time, they discover that overseas development does not provide the cost advantage they had anticipated. Naturally, they become disillusioned.

On the other hand, successful companies have quite a different orientation. They understand that thinking solely in terms of outsource, offshore, and cost is a sure way to create divisions and ineffectiveness.

Instead of thinking to send offshore or to outsource, successful companies ask such questions as, "How do we distribute our development efforts to take advantage of geographical differences in skills and costs to meet customer requirements in a more effective manner?"

These companies have built and continue to successfully operate world-class offshore development operations, in which cost reduction is just one of many advantages. The companies recognized from the start that this is a significant multi-disciplinary effort requiring top-level commitment to succeed.

Motorola set up its own subsidiary in India in the early 90s, which has become one of the few organizations in the world with SEI level 5 certification. Beyond cost, the processes and quality initiatives that were developed offshore have benefited the rest of the organization.

FROM THE TRENCHES

Establish project selection criteria

Set up and follow pre-set criteria for projects/products based on overall strategic objectives. Select projects that provide the most leverage and keep both the domestic and the overseas work forces challenged. Here is a list of considerations:

♦ Clearly definable deliverables
♦ Manageable level of interface to other groups in the company
♦ Good skill match
♦ Compliant with export control regulations
♦ Favorable financial analysis
♦ Maintainability of equipment outside the U.S.
♦ Availability of personnel in the U.S. organization for transfer of technology
♦ Training time
♦ Risk containment
♦ Retention of offshore talent

The company's development backlog will influence how to leverage overseas resources. Some companies have a large queue of planned development projects. Their work force clearly welcomes any relief.

On the other hand, other companies have a limited amount of new development. The dilemma faced by these managers is how to increase overseas development while maintaining the morale of the work force in their "primary" country. This is a difficult management task.

Utilizing resources overseas solely for enhancement or support work means that the primary advantage is cost. If overseas cost structures change in the future, this advantage is likely to decrease.

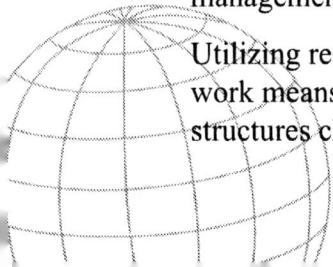

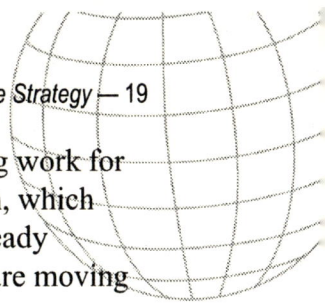

In addition, if the company does not provide challenging work for the overseas work force, it may create a morale problem, which can create turnover since dozens of companies have already realized the potential of the worldwide work force and are moving in that direction.

Through careful planning, a company might be able to turn this challenge to an advantage. Being able to properly leverage the work force abroad in order to bring new products to market faster will likely improve the position of the company in the market. In that way it might be able to use overseas development to actually enhance the overall competitiveness, which should benefit all employees.

You can assess the likelihood of whether a particular project is a candidate for offshore development by filling out the following Project Selection Score Card template illustrated in Figure 1.

Criteria	Score
Definable Deliverables	
Level of Interface	
Skill Match	
Exportability	
ROI	
Equipment	
TOI	
Training	
Risk	
Retention of offshore talent	
Total	

Figure 1 — Project Selection Score Card

In order to identify a good candidate for offshore development, a company can customize the above template for its specific needs. By assigning a score of 1 to 5 to each attribute, you can quickly see if a project makes sense.

Determine the form of organization

One early decision companies face is whether to work alone or with a local partner. If the company is not sure of the direction, using a local partner gives the company time to experiment with the concept without total commitment.

There is a continuum of increasing risks going from sub-contracting to complete ownership.

Organizational options

Two distinct forms of relationships when working with another company include:

♦ Outsourcing to sub-contractors.
♦ Forming a strategic alliance with a longer-term orientation.

If it wishes, the company can have ownership in the entity in three ways:

1. Joint venture with a partner
2. Wholly owned subsidiary
3. Build-Operate-Transfer (BOT)

Outsourcing to Subcontractors

Outsourcing to a subcontractor is the model in which a specified piece of work (a task or a project) is given to a company, which delivers the end results. Outsourcing has a "procurement" orientation. No long-term commitment is required from either side.

Outsourcing can be used effectively for only short duration development efforts. However, this works well in cases where everything can be well specified ahead of time. Examples are data entry, conversions, and possibly porting. Cost reduction and access to additional bandwidth are the primary goals.

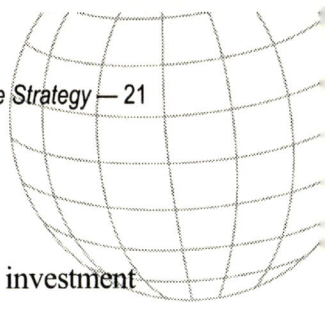

Advantages	◆ Can get started quickly.
	◆ No long term commitment.
Disadvantages	◆ Must be able to justify recovering the investment on a per project basis.
	◆ Investment in knowledge transfers will be short-lived.

Strategic Alliances

An alternative to outsourcing is to establish strategic alliances with the right company or companies, depending upon the situation. Three key differences compared to the subcontracting model include commitment for longer term, visibility, and sharing of each other's strategies.

Advantages	Strategic alliances offer the flexibility to pick the best in class, provides the best fit (from a cultural and long term strategy perspective) for the two companies, and reduces start up time. Other benefits include:
	◆ Local issues to be handled by the local partner.
	◆ Flexibility in staffing levels.
Challenges	◆ Not 100% company specific.
	◆ Must share profits with partner.
	◆ Partner priorities may change over time.
	◆ Investments made in people/infrastructure that are not a company's own.
	◆ Dependence on the partner.
	◆ Alignment of partner's employees with the parent company's strategy.

Concerning this last point, the staff will operate at a less than effective level if team members feel that the work they are doing does not further their careers.

Joint Venture

A joint venture is a legal entity in which each participant owns a percentage of the joint entity. Each invests money, management, equipment, technology, etc., in the common entity and shares risks and rewards. The joint venture provides the ability for both partners to receive benefits that could not be derived by independent action.

A joint venture can permit more control than a strategic alliance, but it requires a longer lead-time to become operational. A joint venture permits much less flexibility in managing the level of work force and also requires a long-term commitment.

Advantages The main advantage of a joint venture is in ownership and control. A company can exercise control if it owns a majority of the joint venture. One of the motivations for companies to go overseas is to gain access to the talent pool. Being able to control the operation means that the U.S. company has a direct say in how the talent pool is managed.

Other advantages include:

- ♦ Risks can be shared.
- ♦ Better ownership of intellectual property.
- ♦ Easier to have the entity do critical projects than in outsourcing or strategic alliances.
- ♦ The organization can be developed faster because:
    - ♦ The offshore partner provides infrastructure for dealing with local issues such as building, electricity, phones, relationships with local governmental entities, and other businesses that facilitates a faster start.
    - ♦ The offshore partner provides the entity with people having the right skill sets and with processes already in place, which will reduce the recruiting and training cycle.

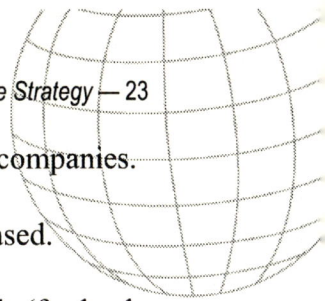

Challenges
- Managing the expectations of both companies.
- Speed of decision making.
- Time to implement is usually increased.
- Longer term commitment.
- Flexibility in handling staffing levels (for load leveling) is reduced.
- Benefits must be shared between the U.S. company and the offshore partner.
- Unless you specifically arrange it, the joint venture might not be dedicated to only one U.S. company — in this case a company may be creating an entity that its competition can take advantage of.

Advantages for the off- shore joint venture partner
- The other partner brings money needed to undertake the activity.
- The other partner brings in management know how, which will expand the management bandwidth and/or provide the offshore partner with viewpoints that may not exist internally.
- The other partner brings in technology that does not exist and hence improves the technology base of the offshore partner.

Wholly owned subsidiary

Advantages
- Able to control the offshore organization in the same way as the rest of the company.
- Able to distribute work among various entities.
- More easily able to carry out critical projects offshore (compared to non-ownership models).
- Receive 100% of the benefits.
- Better ownership of intellectual property.
- Can readily transfer corporate culture to the offshore location.

Challenges
♦ Time to implement can be longer than other models.
♦ Requires greater investment.
♦ Requires more lengthy commitment.
♦ Reduces flexibility in handling permanent staff (because of local laws).
♦ Requires a management team that understands the local culture in order to attract and retain the necessary talent.
♦ Requires running a company overseas.

Employee turnover will increase if a company neglects the final point. Overseas employees must be managed the same way as local employees —for example, in the career path available for them.

Build-Operate-Transfer (BOT)

In this model the U.S. company engages a partner offshore to establish the operation, operate it for a period of time and then have it transferred to the U.S. company as a wholly owned subsidiary.

Many mid-sized companies and some start-ups focused on product development offshore are attracted to this because of intellectual property issues. Such companies wish to own the operation, but generally lack the know how, contacts, or management bandwidth to do it at the outset. In the case of startups, during the initial stages ownership of the offshore entity may not be important. However, as they approach IPO, they may need to show that they control their resources and intellectual property.

The BOT approach provides these types of companies a way to reach their objectives.

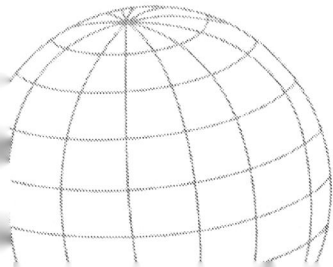

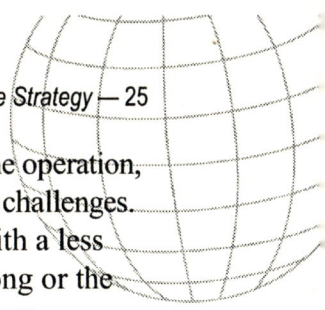

Advantages

♦ Apparent advantages of possessing the operation, without immediate ownership and its challenges.

♦ A "try before you buy" approach with a less costly exit strategy, if things go wrong or the need for offshore operation goes away.

♦ Potential for faster start compared to establishing the company's own operation from the beginning, since it leverages partner's infrastructure, processes, and people.

♦ Better management of intellectual property.

♦ Provides more influence on the operation of the entity.

♦ Can exercise the option to acquire the operation.

Challenges

♦ Partner selection is more challenging. (The number of companies who have successfully executed this is smaller compared to strategic alliances.)

♦ Potential partners must be investigated thoroughly and due diligence exercised since partners must clearly understand what is involved and what they are actually willing and able to execute.

♦ Transfer pricing issues must be addressed in a way satisfactory to both parties. (A BOT has the characteristics of an acquisition, but projections can prove challenging.)

♦ People management issues will be challenging since at the outset they must operate under the policies of the partner, but one day they will be transferred to the U.S. operation.

♦ Must have clear understanding of how the operation will be run — what the partner will do and what the company will do.

♦ The partner may not give this segment of his company the same attention, since it might be seen as a temporary management contract.

These approaches are not mutually exclusive. Some companies combine approaches. Companies have a definite orientation towards a specific model based on the company's philosophy. For example some companies simply will not consider anything other than a subsidiary for their core technology areas.

The right answer for a company depends on its own situation. The key is for management to think through these options. Then it will be able to structure the operation from the start to provide a migration path as confidence in the operation increases and willingness to take more risk is accepted.

◆ Texas Instruments set up its own subsidiary in India, which initially engaged in product development. The organization subsequently has gone on to selling and supporting products.

FROM THE TRENCHES

◆ Oracle set up its own subsidiary in India.

◆ Verifone (which was acquired by HP) and Novell worked with local partners for a while before setting up their own operations.

◆ Agile set up its own operation in India from the beginning.

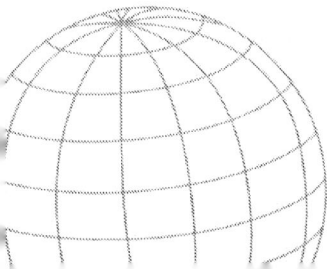

Select country for best long term fit

One of the early tasks when embarking on offshore development is to decide what country or countries to operate in. Consider the following list of factors to consider when comparing countries.

- *Expected role:* i.e., of the country in the global economy over the next decade.
- *Type of business opportunities the country offers:* Whether market potential, leveraging of skill-set, or both. Determine the regions of the country that are most likely to have potential for meeting the business objectives.
- *Business climate and prevailing view:* i.e., towards the nationality of the participant.
- *The global citizenship of the country:* How it may affect doing business there.
- *Export control:* Regulations may affect sending equipment and or technology to that country.
- *Political stability in the country:* This will influence the decision of whether to do business in this country, and if so, the type of work.
- *Talent pool available:* Estimate size of the available talent pool and competition for the talent. Dig deeper to understand the specific talent available for your company's needs. For example, if the company needs personnel with skill set in networking, the general number of developers available in the country is not a good enough indicator.
- *Ability to ramp up:* Assuming that a talent pool is available, the company must understand how fast it can ramp up the operation. It must determine if the ability to ramp up matches its particular needs.
- *Start-up time:* This takes into account all issues to consider in starting up an operation in a particular country. Depending on regulations and infrastructure, start-up time can vary widely.
- *Determine costs beyond salaries.* This should include the additional costs incurred in the headquarters in order to set up and manage the operation.

♦ *Infrastructure availability:* Undertaking development projects abroad requires access to communications for data transfer, electricity, space, backup facilities for business continuity, and other infrastructure needs.

♦ *Required management skills:* Availability of management talent is a key consideration. The company can hire and train individual contributors in technology areas, but management development takes longer. Plan to hire local managers as much as possible.

♦ *Language skills:* Even though English has become the link language in global business, not every country speaks English. Translating will slow down transactions and will influence the type of work a company can do in a particular country. It may be possible to undertake some longer cycle projects but may be difficult for projects requiring a short turn around.

One technique effective in evaluating offshore resources is to send a cross-functional team of senior personnel to the countries of potential interest for on-site fact finding. Team members should include expertise in:

FROM THE TRENCHES

♦ Subject matter — i.e., development, support, IT, BPO, etc.

♦ Knowledge about the country's business practices and culture

♦ Industry contacts in the country under consideration

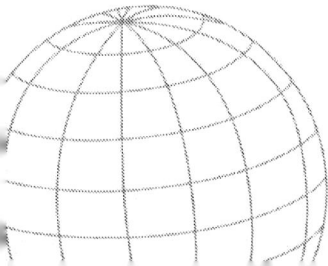

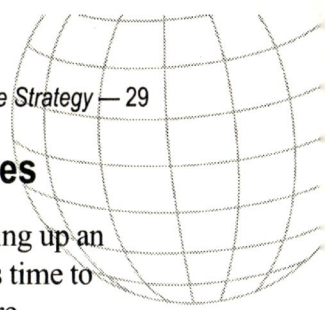

Determine entire cost, not just salaries

The company must take into account the entire cost of setting up an offshore development facility and not salaries only. It takes time to gain a good understanding of the overall cost of the offshore organization. Companies that understand this will be better equipped to compare costs rationally. Specific costs to consider include:

- ◆ Communications
  - Phone
  - Data communications
  - Travel
  - Email
  - Video
- ◆ Potential over-estimation of offshore productivity
- ◆ Potential under-estimation of labor cost at the offshore location
- ◆ Additional required management at the U.S. company
- ◆ Cost of vendor selection or setting up your own operation
- ◆ Cost of training/transfer of information
- ◆ Cost of organizational change, for example layoffs
- ◆ Potential duplication of resources

Concerning the final point, in some projects, the company may need to duplicate the equipment — i.e., provide the same equipment in both locations, which will increase the investment in equipment involved in going offshore.

Establish major milestones

From the beginning, the company must have a clear-cut idea of the expected size of the operation and how the company plans to achieve that growth.

Planning should include defining specific projects and head count for year one and forecasts for years two and three.

Major milestones must be established so that management can develop financial forecasts and track progress.

Develop a multi-year financial analysis

A realistic assessment of financial benefits requires projection to three years to allow enough time for reaching critical mass and stability of operations. This analysis should provide an understanding of cost savings, investment, return on investment (ROI), and cash flow.

Select a strategy to gain momentum

In some organizations offshore development is readily understood and supported. If you are that lucky, you can skip this section. However, many organizations have a reluctance to try offshore development.

In order to overcome organizational inertia in attempting offshore development for the first time, the company may need to establish explicit strategies. Approaches that have been tried include:

- ◆ Funding initial development at the corporate level instead of asking a specific department to fund out of its own budget.

- ◆ Setting goals for the current organization to reduce development cost without reducing the amount of work. This will force them to use the offshore development facility, since they may be able to "do more with less."

Following one or another of these approaches will allow the offshore organization to focus its attention on developing infrastructure and other issues rather than on obtaining business during the early phase of the effort. However, once past this stage, most companies require the offshore organization to compete for business, which keeps them from becoming complacent.

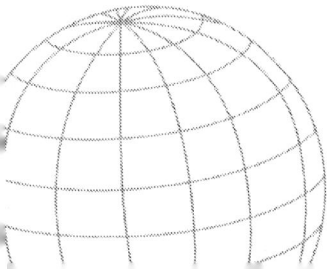

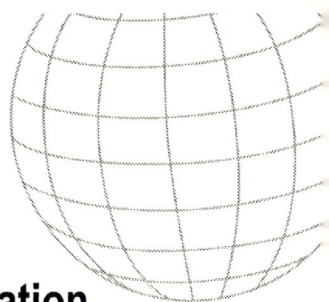

CHAPTER FOUR

Create a Single Networked Organization

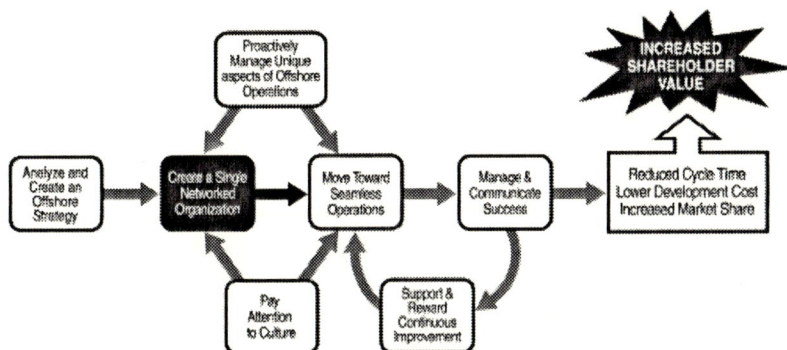

Rather than setting up offshore organizations as silos, set up a single networked organization. People offshore need to feel that they are an integral part of the U.S. company. Reinforcing a sense of belonging and importance promotes unity and cultural understanding, and maximizes productivity.

If you decide to use partners, select the right partners to meet the company's goals. Some partners may have the ability to take your business up a notch due to their unique value add.

This chapter presents two organizational models and criteria for selecting partners.

Best practices

- ◆ Create an integrated organization.
- ◆ If partners are required, find and select those who will capitalize on unique global capabilities for skill set, cost, and cultural fit.

Create an integrated organization

Every high impact offshore development effort requires contributions from a variety of functions across the company, including product development, quality assurance, release processes, logistics support, telecommunications, contracting, public relations, training, finance, and development processes. Explicit policies about ownership and accountability must be well understood.

The offshore development organization, which will have a U.S. component and an offshore component, must be staffed with personnel who have the ability to create linkages between organizations to deal with issues, to plan effectively, and to make day-to-day decisions. Creating cross-functional virtual teams provides a means to achieve this objective.

In addition to the subject knowledge that a cross functional virtual team brings to the organization, such a team also provides the ability to network quickly with members of the organization who have to participate in or support actions that need to be taken.

When using a partnership business model, this networking ability should extend not only throughout each organization, but also interconnect both organizations with each other.

Below are two examples based on our observations in the field.

Divisional Ownership model

Each of the divisions or the operating entities continues to "own" the products/projects that are handled offshore. The central coordination function typically deals with relationship, business, infrastructure, and best practices. Divisional program/project managers report to their respective line organizations.

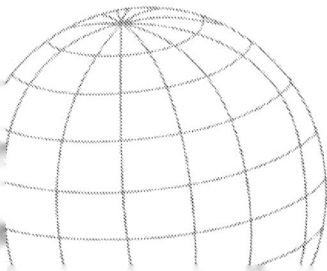

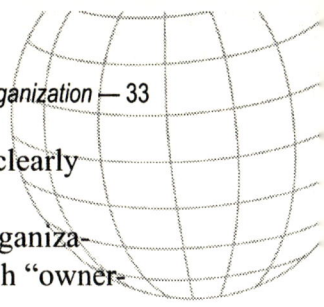

Advantages

- Ownership of deliverables is clearly defined.
- The operating entities (line organizations) do not need to relinquish "ownership" of the projects.
- Functional areas have the required depth of knowledge to continue to provide strategic direction.
- Organizational change is minimized.
- The tendency to send "less desirable" projects offshore is reduced (since the same organization continues to be responsible for the products).

Disadvantages

- Tendency to create organizational silos offshore paralleling the divisional boundaries of the headquarters.
- Difficulty increased for the offshore organization to balance workload and skill sets.
- Increased difficulty in requiring the partner to satisfy multiple parties.
- Creates necessity for each division at the headquarters to buy into offshore strategy.

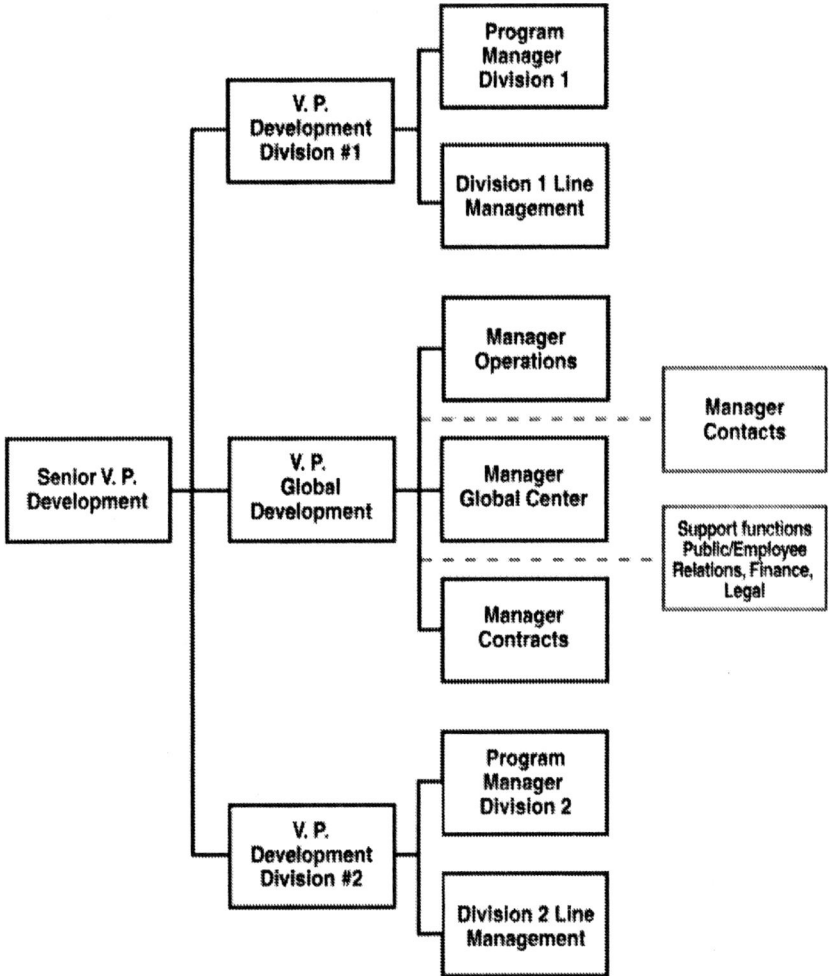

Figure 2 — Organization chart — Divisional Ownership

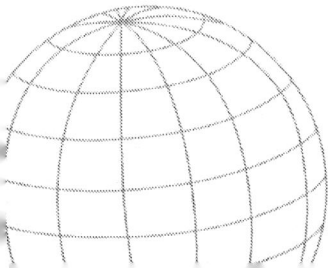

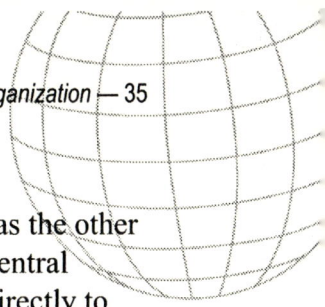

Central Ownership model

In this model the responsibility for deliverables as well as the other functions of central coordination are transferred to the central organization. The divisional program managers report directly to one central offshore manager.

Advantages
- Total responsibility for success of the offshore effort resides in one place.
- Much easier to allocate and balance resources.
- Easier to manage relationship with the offshore entity, establish processes, and handle infrastructure.

Disadvantages
- Higher tendency to send offshore projects that product divisions do not want to keep, especially those that are older and only require sustaining.
- Reduced sense of ownership by product divisions for specific projects/products.
- Increased potential for fragmented and unclear lines of responsibility for product areas.
- Technical expertise resides in other organizations.

That last point is especially difficult. People who built these products and now want to build new products will want to be in the product divisions. This increases the difficulty of managing plans for these products in the long term.

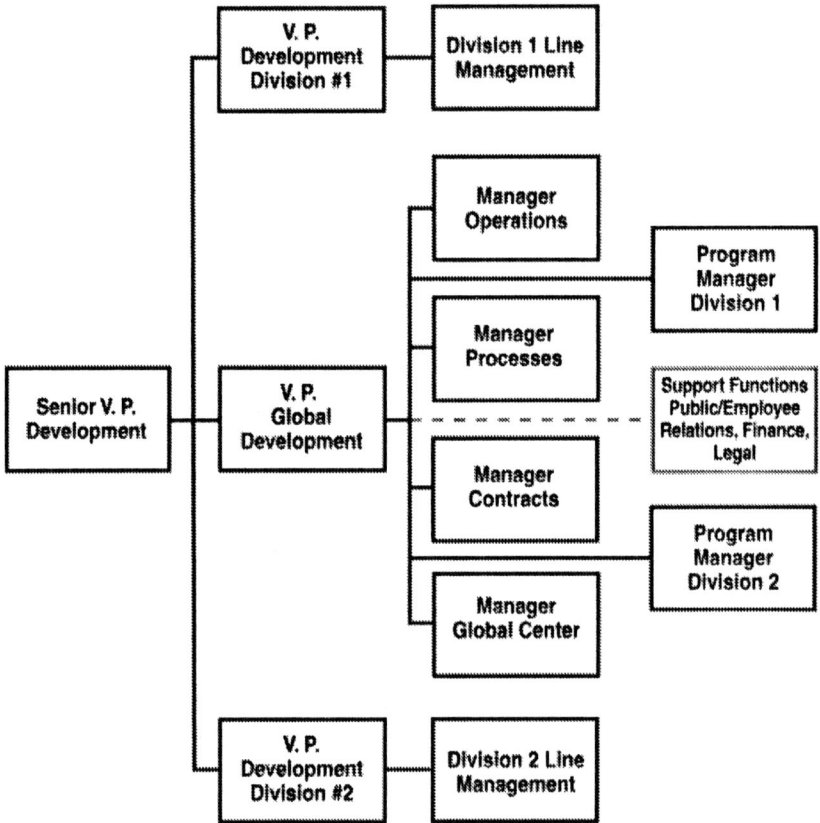

Figure 3 — Organizational Chart — Central Ownership

The Divisional Ownership approach is often more successful during the early stages of a development effort. A key aspect is the continued ownership of products by the current organization while it is still engaged in building the offshore development organization (overseas facilities, processes, and infrastructure to name a few areas).

Once a development operation has stabilized, the company may consider assessing the need for some other approach.

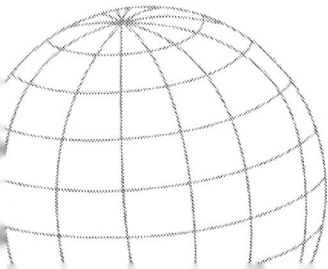

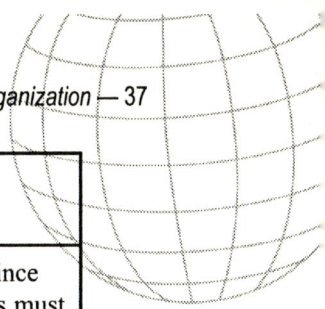

	Divisional Ownership	Central Ownership
Organizational change	None to minimal	Can be high, since current projects must be transferred to offshore organization
Ownership of projects	Stays with the corresponding line organization	Transferred; can lead to turf issues
Impact on project selection	None	Tendency to dump obsolete products
Technical depth	Stays the same	Likely to get diluted
Balancing of offshore resources	Can be difficult because of the potential for offshore silos	Easier
Relationship management with offshore entities	Challenging since multiple divisions are involved	Easier
Responsibility for product areas	Stays the same; provides product line focus	Potential for divided responsibility
Strategic direction for the product	Stays the same	Increased difficulty

Figure 4 — Comparison of the two organizational models

Select right partners

Any decision to work with another company (which is the case with all business models except wholly owned subsidiary) requires careful selection of the partner to best fit the requirements of the situation.

The factors

The following factors are important when choosing a partner:

Relationship, trust, and cooperation   It is not always possible to specify every detail in contracts covering development in complex technology areas. Mutual cooperation and trusting relationships are required at all levels of the organization, which will facilitate mutually satisfactory resolutions of the issues that will undoubtedly come up.

For example, relationships based on confidence and trust between the organizations will smooth the implementation of any required reduction of work offshore, regardless of what the contract specifies.

Corporate Culture   Every company over a period of time will develop a definite culture. Of all the factors, this is the hardest to change. For example, the culture of a product development company is different from that of an IT services company.

Flexibility   Technologies and business conditions are both changing rapidly so all arrangements must be flexible. The partner must adhere to the original arrangement but be willing to deal with change in a professional manner.

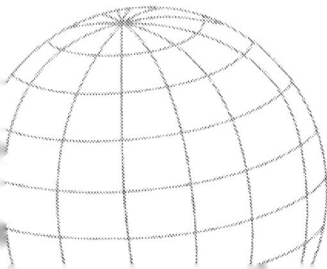

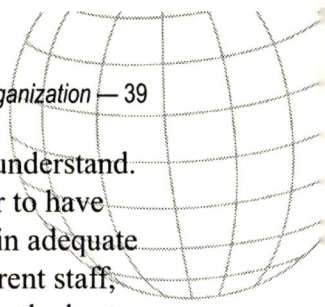

Skill set/technical expertise	This is the most visible and easiest to understand. It is imperative for the offshore partner to have adequate depth of technical skills and in adequate numbers. In addition to examining current staff, the partner's ability to attract and retain the best talent in the country should be examined. What campuses do they recruit from? What is the caliber of their graduates? What is their reputation in university recruitment circles?
Partner references	Past performance provides a good indication of how they may perform the current task. The company should thoroughly examine U.S. customer references of the potential offshore partners in order to assess their actual capabilities.
Ability to handle local issues	The offshore partner should know its way around the local governmental bureaucracy. Such knowledge can make the difference between a project that takes weeks versus months.
Price	The company must understand the total cost a partner is charging, not just the direct cost of the people doing the work.
Influence on the partner	The U.S. company must understand how important its business will be to the partner. For example, if a company's business represents 30% of the offshore organization's revenues, the offshore company will look at the U.S. company differently than it would if it is 5%. Don't forget that if your company provides 30% of the offshore organization's business, and then the level of business with them needs to be reduced, the stability of the partner organization may come into question. For this reason, some offshore companies have a policy of not taking more than 10% of their business from one customer.

Business Practices	Business practices vary from country to country and from one offshore company to another. The U.S. company should develop a clear understanding of the business practices of the potential partner and their impact, if any.
Stability of partner	The company must understand a potential partner's finances and background of key management personnel to assess if it will be stable through economic cycles.
Customer relationship	The partner's track record.
Business models	Whether this is T&M, fixed price, or any variation, the company should assure itself that the two organizations are in alignment.
Infrastructure	In addition to computers, communication, and physical plant, the company must assure itself that the partner has developed sufficient infrastructure and has put in place disaster recovery and business continuity processes. (This issue has taken on more prominence since the 9/11 incident.)
Retention of knowledge base	In most cases, there will be knowledge transfer from the U.S. company to the partner company. It is crucial to understand the track record of people turnover and what knowledge retention mechanisms are in place. Otherwise, knowledge base can erode, impacting quality and causing delays in schedules.
Unique value add by the partner	A company should extend its search for partners beyond those who can merely extend the volume of what the company is currently doing or do it for less. Both capabilities have an impact primarily only on cost. Instead, identify partners who can add unique value to your business, thereby taking your business up a notch.

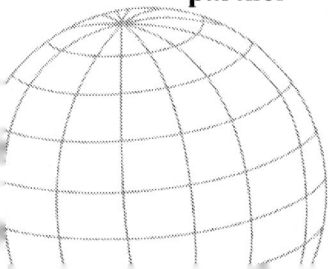

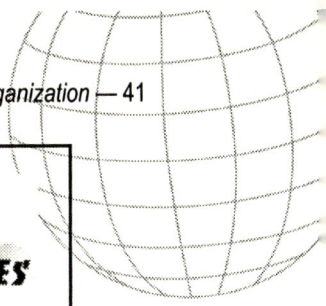

One company we surveyed approached their market exactly as we've been describing. It is leveraging core competencies offshore while minimizing its own investments.

FROM THE TRENCHES

The company manufactures Digital Signal Processors (DSPs) and provides support to OEMs who can incorporate them into their products — much like any other processor vendor. But, the pace of usage is limited since the cost of developing software for various applications requires expensive human resources.

To deal with this issue, the company identified several organizations around the world, comprising some universities and some small, innovative development shops. The company then succeeded in getting these entities to develop algorithms and software based on their own core competence either through small financing or promise of royalties.

One of the organizations, for example, developed modem software, another speech compression, a third MPEG2, and a fourth developed ISDN.

The required cost and time for development, using this plan, will be much less than the costs of the parent organization doing everything by itself. As a direct result of its distributed win-win development model, the company has a highly competitive product and is confident of selling large numbers of its DSPs.

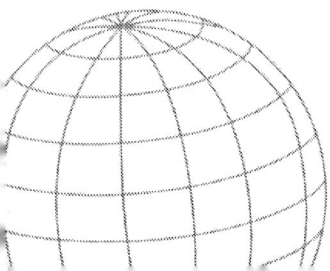

CHAPTER FIVE

Move Toward Seamless Operations

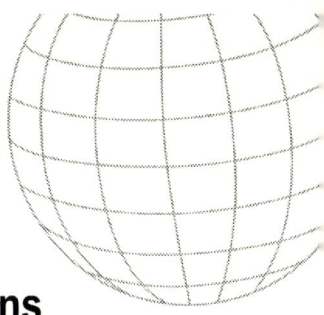

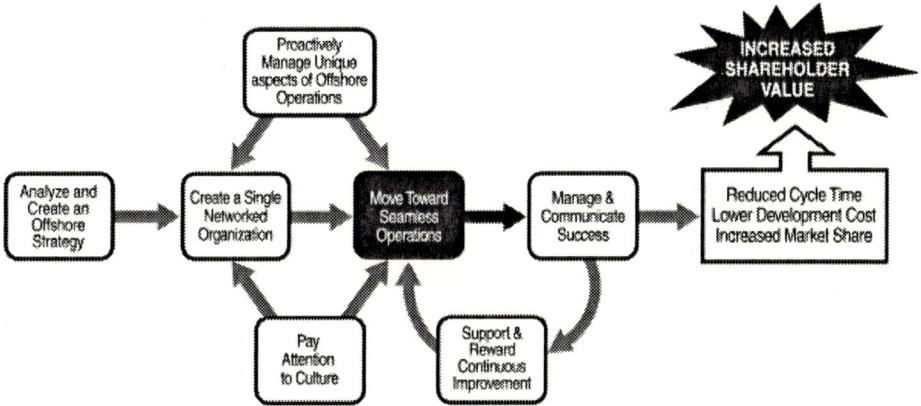

Regardless of form of ownership, offshore development must join two teams in a complimentary relationship that will operate as a single seamless organization.

It is crucial for both management personnel and development personnel to have easy access to one another and communicate effectively.

Best practices

- ♦ Install timely, context-driven communication
- ♦ Provide tools for communication and collaboration
- ♦ Empower teams with information and authority
- ♦ Assure people mobility

Install timely, context-driven communication

Communication in both directions is important, and should be timely and context driven. Bad news looks worse when viewed at a distance.

Since teams located far from each other may not have the same context as those that are co-located, both parties need to provide the right context for the other.

Offshore partners often pass information to the other party (who may be located thousands of miles away in a different time zone and culture) on the assumption that the recipient knows the context. This can cause misunderstandings in some cases, or delays in others since the receiving party is forced to seek clarification before acting on the information.

The type of miscommunication described above can be corrected if the receiver of the message has the right context or the sender provides it before conveying the message. This holds true for communication on any media - email, telephone, etc. Two-way communication media, such as telephone or video, offer the advantage of providing the receiver opportunity to ask questions when the context is not obvious.

♦ Frequent communications will help maintain synchronization in changing environments. Project managers in successful companies conduct regular visits to the offshore facility. In between visits these managers augment communication by utilizing the communication tools presented later in this section.

♦ Some companies choose to relocate key personnel abroad for specified periods to handle this function.

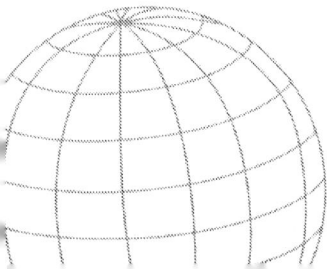

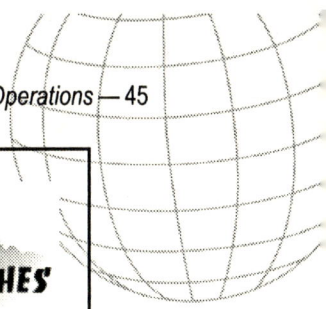

Timely communications take on a crucial role when the headquarters engineering staff in a company integrates the components of a product, part of which may be built or maintained offshore.

FROM THE TRENCHES

In one instance a development manager in the U.S. is responsible to manage an offshore team and to be the point person for the product line in release meetings at which schedules of various components are discussed. The manager remarked

> "It is a good thing I have sensitized my offshore team to what I have to deal with when I go into these meetings. It is simply unacceptable to report to the Vice President chairing these meetings with lack of status information. I needed to know in great detail exactly what progress is being made, what the issues are and what help, if any, the offshore team needed."

Provide tools for communication and collaboration

Commonly used tools include:

Teleconferences Regular teleconferences become an essential part of a distributed operation.

Videoconference Videoconferences can be effectively used to supplement travel, which can be a significant advantage when dealing with high-context cultures.

Web-based conference solutions have improved both in quality and cost in recent years. Depending on the particular situation, a company can buy these services or, if it prefers, can set up its own dedicated facility.

Data links When faced with security and speed requirements, deploy dedicated data links. (Otherwise, you can use the Internet to transfer files.)

Voice over IP   With the advent of voice over IP, the cost of phone calls and videoconferences is changing rapidly. Voice quality may be poor on the public network, but some companies are making bandwidth on their own dedicated network available for voice over IP. In these cases the quality is good and the incremental expense is effectively zero, since the network is already in place for data.

Collaboration tools   Recent advances in technology have provided Internet-based tools that enable collaboration and reduce the feeling of separation. Virtually everything a person could do in a face-to-face meeting can be done on a remote basis.

♦ One company has set up a truly distributed environment, with facilities around the world that have a common "look and feel." In addition, the communication systems are set up to operate the same way in every location. They have implemented "local dialing" capability which greatly facilitates peer to peer communication. For example, employees can dial a specific phone number (54756) from any location in the world wide organization and get the same party.

♦ A variation of this approach used by another company is to set up an 800 number for the main campus. Any party from anywhere in the U.S. can call that number, then dial the 5-digit number to reach an offshore location.

♦ The offshore operation and the U.S. operation will be in different time zones and the amount of overlap will vary. This is important for personnel who need to conduct teleconferences or videoconferences. For instance, a company on the West Coast of the U.S. could be looking at a 12-hour time difference. This means that either the U.S. team and/or the offshore team will have to work outside "normal" working hours. This will be an ongoing operational issue.

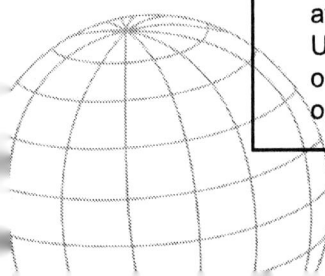

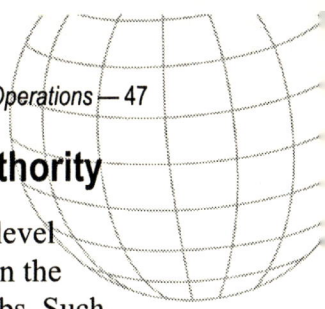

Empower teams with information and authority

In the best companies, decision making is at the lowest level possible where information resides. Teams must be given the information and authority necessary to carry out their jobs. Such empowerment assumes increased importance for offshore teams since time and distance issues generate a natural tendency for delays in decision making. Giving offshore teams information and authority counteracts the effect of these time and distance issues.

Teams empowered in these ways can provide day-to-day operational guidance across functional activities, which includes planning, tracking, technical issues, etc.

Here is an example of how an operational issue is addressed based on information and authority given to the offshore team.

FROM THE TRENCHES

For products that are already out in the field, this company receives "Problem Reports" any time a customer experiences a difficulty; this can be a bug in the product. A severity of 1, 2, or 3 is assigned to each, with 3 being a critical issue. The maximum response time requirement is eight hours.

The offshore team normally has a backlog of work on Severity 1 and 2 issues. However, when a severity 3 issue reaches them, they stop work on severity 1 and 2 issues, address the severity 3 issue, and then return to the severity 1 and 2 issues. The shifts happen in real time without requiring approval or intervention from head quarters.

Assure people mobility

Offshore development assumes the mobility of people involved in the project. Consulates around the world who grant travel visas react not only to current laws and regulations, but also to public sentiment, which can change quite rapidly. Project managers must constantly stay updated on visa regulations. Since 9/11 this issue has taken on increased significance.

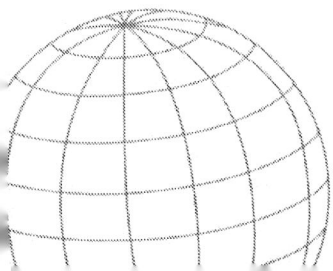

CHAPTER SIX

Proactively Manage Unique Aspects of Offshore Operations

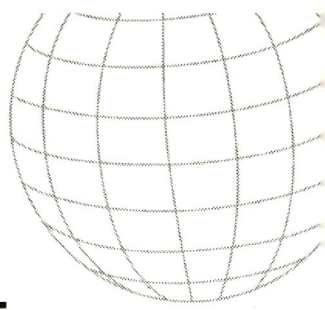

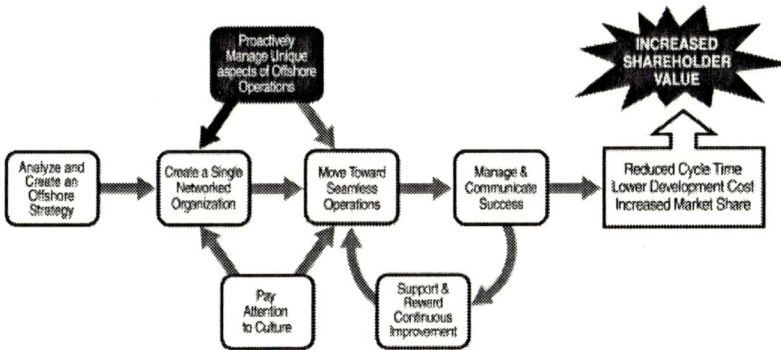

It is essential to put in place several management disciplines that are unique to offshore development. Best practices include:

- ◆ Plan for export control compliance
- ◆ Be prepared for offshore team structure to be different
- ◆ Thoroughly manage technology transfer
- ◆ Retain essential knowledge
- ◆ Provide supplementary project management
- ◆ Install measurement and control systems
- ◆ Install effective change control
- ◆ Manage project risks proactively
- ◆ Protect intellectual property
- ◆ Establish processes for security and continuity
- ◆ Account for variations in operating environment
- ◆ Establish customer relationships protocol
- ◆ Create a best practices document
- ◆ Establish and manage relationships

Plan for export control compliance

The Commerce and State departments set up regulations on the products companies can export to certain countries. Certain types of computers and encryption schemes, for example, currently fall under the prohibited category. The list of prohibited exports continues to change. Companies exporting software or hardware must ensure that they are compliant with all applicable regulations.

Ensuring compliance can become a complex challenge — particularly for a company that is establishing a networked organization with data links providing access to the company's facilities in the U.S. The company may need to re-engineer its processes (and control the level of access provided to offshore personnel) to ensure compliance.

Be prepared for offshore team structure to be different

In the U.S. you can find personnel with deep experience in a specific technology. However, offshore, you are more likely to find generalists. For example, a U.S. group of 10 developers may consist of 5 with 10 years experience, 2 to 3 with 6 to 7 years experience and the rest with lesser years of experience. You are unlikely to be able to replicate this experience mix offshore; you may find the leader of the group with 5 to 6 years experience and the rest with lesser levels of experience.

You should not plan on one to one transfer at the individual level, but transfer at the group level. You may need to restructure how the work is organized based on the skill levels. As the industry matures offshore, this situation may change. But for the near future, you need to take this factor into account.

Thoroughly manage technology transfer

Technology transfer is a key challenge in establishing an offshore development facility, and in high technology areas, can be difficult, time consuming, and complex.

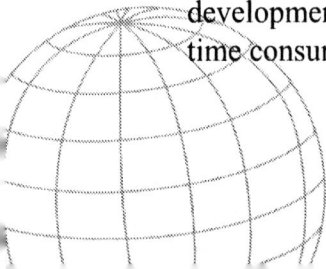

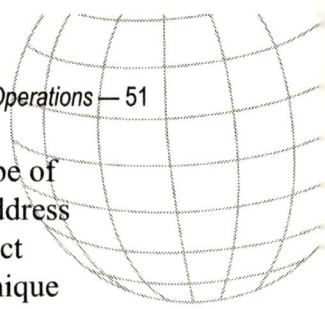

- The company must recognize the full scope of the challenge and put together a plan to address aspects of the transfer beyond mere product knowledge. Such a plan should include unique processes and other related areas to enable the offshore unit to become fully functional.
- Beyond the initial transfer, a plan should identify processes to keep the teams continuously updated.
- A transfer plan might include a "train the trainer" component, which can help manage costs and schedules.
- A technology transfer plan should also include "hands on training." For example, a transfer plan for a development project might include a component in which trainees actually fix bugs.

An approach frequently used in technology transfers is to have the offshore team work side by side with the U.S. personnel for a period of time to learn the technology and processes. If properly managed, the teams will establish personal linkages and rapport so that mutual trust is built and progress is made toward creating a single organization — in addition to simply carrying out the transfer of technical knowledge.

What follows is the case study of a team that used a structured training approach to reduce by two-thirds the time required for technology transfer:

The offshore development project team consisted of 12 developers from three different cultures (U.S., India, and China). The team faced the challenge of receiving technology for a complex set of five operating system related products. The team would then use the technology to enhance the product line. No one on the team had any prior experience with the products.

It was crucial for the team to thoroughly understand existing products before designing enhancements. The normal training time to attain this level of proficiency was 9 to 12 months. The team was able to shorten the training cycle to about three months.

The team was initially given classroom training for about a month. Then the members were tasked to study product details. The five products were divided among members of the team so that each product had two developers assigned to it. They also divided the product into segments so that each member had a specific part of the product to deal with.

During this phase of the transfer, developers would conclude each day's activities by taking turns to explain to the rest of the team members what they had learned about their assigned area that day. After each report, the team member was questioned and challenged by the rest of the team.

This approach created a non-threatening learning environment. By the time each discussion ended, the presenter, as well as the rest of the team, had a good understanding of that particular technology segment.

Besides providing a forum for learning, this process was instrumental in developing a superior team spirit. The technology transfer phase forged the group into a technically competent, effective, and cohesive team.

Each team member knew the knowledge domain of all the others. During the remainder of the project, which lasted about one year, when someone had a question, he knew exactly who to turn to. Resolution of issues that might have required days or weeks was accomplished in minutes or hours.

Retain essential knowledge

Offshore development projects involve distributing important corporate assets, including knowledge of technology, processes, and products. Turnover of personnel at either the headquarters or offshore will degrade these assets.

The headquarters often re-deploys people for other work immediately after transferring a project offshore. Offshore turnover also occurs due to market conditions or because the partner maintains a policy of short interval rotation of people.

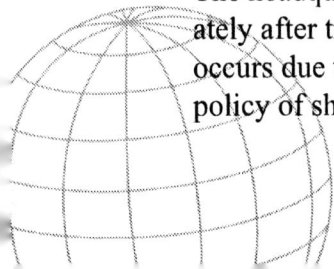

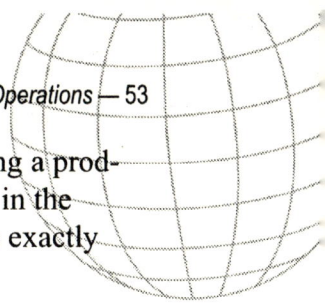

These events can combine to result in a partner delivering a product that does not work — to the bafflement of everyone in the organization, none of whom really knows or remembers exactly what was supposed to happen.

To deal with this effectively, management must acknowledge the issue early, understand the level of turnover to expect, and proactively work to retain and even expand essential knowledge. A company can counteract turnover by:

- ◆ Cross training.
- ◆ Moderate over-staffing in the early phases.
- ◆ Identifying the mix of new development versus maintenance that will be sufficient to retain the work force.
- ◆ Creating effective retention plans (e.g., stock options and incentives).
- ◆ Establishing a pleasant work environment.
- ◆ Updating knowledge capture mechanisms.
- ◆ Preserving core competence at the headquarters.
- ◆ Documenting statements of work, deliverables, and time lines and keeping these current as events force changes in the project. With these in place, it is easier to determine whether the offshore organization is meeting expectations or not.
- ◆ Identifying the level of turnover by developing and gathering metrics.

Provide supplementary project management

Project management competence levels vary widely among various countries and companies. Offshore development magnifies every project management issue. Distance and time differentials can create an "out of sight out of mind" syndrome, which can result in disconnects. Managers do not become aware of problems in a timely fashion and run the risk of learning about issues after savings have disappeared and the project deadline is imminent.

- ◆ Rather than sending the project offshore and leaving it entirely to that organization (especially if it is with a partner), a company should take time to determine the level of project management competence and invest in defenses against delegation without controls, disconnects, and delays. Project management should be assured of excellence at the offshore operation.

♦ In addition, the company can provide supplementary project management by either:
  ♦ Relocating project managers offshore, particularly during the early stages of the effort; or
  ♦ Having project managers travel to the offshore site on a regular basis.

In either case, management should drill down for true versus formal status. They should seek to overcome the natural hierarchical inertia by holding one-on-ones at various levels of organization. This ensures the discovery of what is actually going on versus overly optimistic estimates. Such diligence will also clarify the competency of local project managers, and will highlight what, if anything, needs to be done to augment their skills.

♦ When not traveling to the offshore site, a U.S. manager can still supplement offshore project managers by taking an active part in assessing the progress of projects in order to stay current..

Some U.S. development managers wish to move low activity products offshore — for instance an old release that receives one problem report a month and each problem report takes half a day to fix. They run into a problem of staff and knowledge retention.

FROM THE TRENCHES

For one thing, the partner may not have people with first hand knowledge of the product. Also, it may be difficult for the partner to attract and then retain developers on this low activity product because of their career aspirations. International markets for engineering talent are increasingly competitive and quality of work life is an issue there as well.

On the other hand, if the product is retained by the U.S. company, those who originally developed the product could deal with the required low level maintenance at some level in the organization.

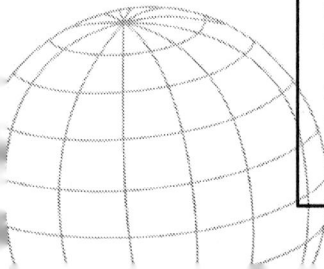

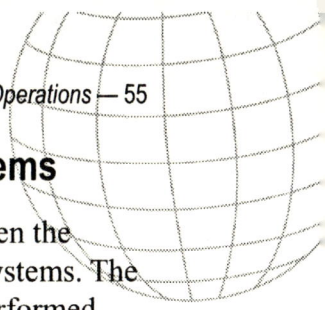

Install measurement and control systems

A major element in building trust and confidence between the entities is to install ongoing measurement and control systems. The offshore organization needs to know when they have performed well. On the other hand, they also must understand what they need to improve. Formal ongoing mechanisms will go a long way towards meeting these two needs.

The requirement for measurement and control is particularly acute during the initial stages, at which point both organizations are developing relationships. Some companies set up specific benchmarks in order to establish a common understanding of what is expected against which performance can be measured.

The process of developing metrics for measurement and control often requires a significant effort. The best companies realize the importance of such metrics, however, and are willing to make the investment. A set of good metrics will provide focus for development efforts. Common examples of such metrics include:

- Schedule
- Cost
- Attrition
- Quality
- Customer satisfaction

Web based project management tools

Rather than having to wait for weekly reports to be delivered to managers' workstations, these tools allow them to monitor progress and view issues from virtually any location around the world. Not only can the team be anywhere in the world, but now the manager can be anywhere in the world as well (not just in his or her office).

◆ One company set up measurement systems to determine the quality, as opposed to the volume of work being done. In this instance quality was critical, so setting up a quality-based measurement and feedback system provided a focus for the organization and also a specific, objective metric that both the U.S. and offshore organizations could look at.

◆ One challenge of metrics is that many U.S. organizations do not have them. It becomes difficult to measure an overseas organization if the U.S. organization itself lacks credible metrics.

Install effective change control

Managers must have good change control practices in place to maintain control over scope, schedule, and cost. Creeping functionality guarantees project failure. Once again, the need for control over adding features is greater in this environment because of time and distance issues.

In any project of appreciable size, requirements are likely to change. The change control process should help all parties understand the impact on both cost and schedules. Often, the offshore organization is not in a position to understand if this change is necessary, because it will not be close enough to the marketplace to understand customers' needs. If an impact assessment shows that a change in requirements is necessary, then a revised schedule and a new cost scenario should be entered into the plan of record.

Offshore organizations can be effective at execution, but the U.S. organization must be sure to address the issue of scope as the project progresses. The project/program manager at the headquarters who is acting as the focal point for technical coordination of the project must constantly monitor scope and handle change control.

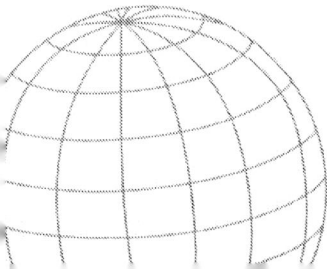

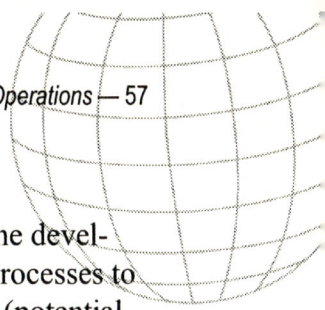

Manage project risks

Risk management practices vary widely depending on the developer, the project, and the manager. Most projects have processes to manage problems (things that are wrong now) and risks (potential future problems). In most cases problems and risks are handled together and current problems get higher priority because of their immediate nature. In most cases, risk management is handled informally. But here is a paradigm that provides a repeatable way for managing risks:

Risk identification	Risks must first be identified. Care must be taken to identify risks before they adversely affect the project. A common way to do this involves individual research, and group meetings.
Risk Analysis	This step analyzes data gathered in the previous step and places the information in the hands of decision-makers.
Risk Planning	Identified risks are prioritized in this step and action plans are developed to address them.
Risk communication	Risks and actions planned must be communicated to appropriate levels in the organization so they can be managed effectively.
Triggers	Triggers for taking action are established.

Turnover is a major risk in any project. As presented earlier, turnover in offshore development can happen for a variety of reasons. Here is how one development team dealt with turn-over risk:

FROM THE TRENCHES

Personnel turnover was identified as a key potential risk at the outset of the project. But the team did not want to add extra personnel, increase cost, and under-utilize some developers. On the other hand, neither did they want to create a possible schedule slip due to training required when someone new entered the project.

To solve the dilemma, the team assigned two developers per product area. Each had a full load to carry, so there was no under-utilization of personnel. Also, each developer had sufficient understanding of the other's area of work so that one of them could be away from the project without losing expertise. Because developers also had expertise in common areas of code across the product line, each had some familiarity with the other's products, which further reduced the risk of turnover.

In addition, the project leader remained very knowledge-able about the technical details of the project so that he could step in and help bring a new person up to speed, without impacting the rest of the staff.

During the two years of development, the team experienced limited turnover. Because of their approach, they were able to bring on new developers while continuing to meet their schedules.

Identifying risks from the inception of a project and developing plans to handle them will greatly enhance a project's ability to maintain schedules. The paradigm presented earlier is one way to approach this issue.

Another approach that can be used in combination with the one described above is to set up rewards and incentives such as stock options and bonuses at the end of the project.

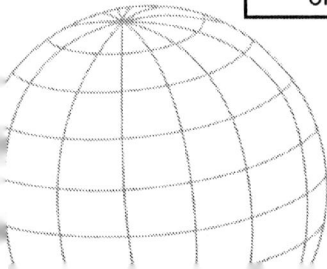

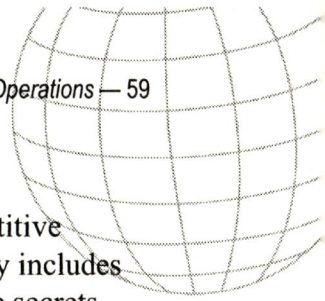

Protect intellectual property

Intellectual property is one of the key sources of competitive advantage in the computer industry. Intellectual property includes copyrights, patents, trade names, and all aspects of trade secrets. The concept of intellectual property protection is not uniformly understood or adhered to around the world.

This issue takes on further importance when you consider the following facts and trends:

♦ Many offshore companies work for a number of customers. It is not uncommon to find that the organization your company wants to work with is also working with your competitor.

An accepted practice in these companies is to rotate development personnel among various projects. This creates a scenario where one of the people who worked on a project may at some time end up working for your competitor, or vice versa.

♦ The computer business is knowledge intensive. Each knowledge worker has access to a "piece" of the technology, with access to not only the documentation, but carrying with him information that is "intellectual property."

♦ Future computer technologies are likely to be developed across borders and each company may own pieces of a technology that only when taken as a whole creates a competitive product.

♦ Given the competitive nature of the industry, the adverse effect on a company can be significant if its intellectual property rights are compromised.

Protecting intellectual property is a multifaceted challenge and must be addressed in that fashion. The issues can be broadly classified in two categories:

♦ Country issues
♦ Organizational issues

Country issues

Offshore development projects encounter two kinds of issues — the country's legal framework and culture.

Legal framework of the country

The law of the land provides the primary legal framework. The country where a company plans to operate must have the legal framework that recognizes intellectual property rights. If this framework does not exist, the other issues become irrelevant.

Timely enforcement of a country's laws is another requirement. A law that is on the books that takes years to enforce is ineffective.

Culture of the country

Laws may exist on books within an essentially lawless culture. If an unwritten cultural standard prevents vigorous enforcement, a law written in a legal code somewhere cannot be of much value. Local practices must be researched to determine if a planned development project will compromise your company's position in the market.

Organizational issues

An organization needs to develop policies and practices for addressing intellectual property issues. Such policies and practices must promote a culture where every one involved is trained to be sensitive to organizational responsibilities.

There has to be clearly understood policy statements specifying both the intent and the practice of guarding intellectual property. A company should consider spelling this out in its contracts.

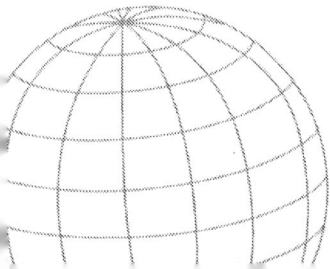

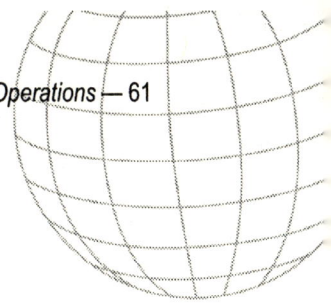

Securing intellectual property involves:

- Physical security
- Training
- Network security
- Individual Compliance
- Individual non-disclosure agreements
- Network security
- Control of access
- Audits

The best form of compliance involves voluntary agreement by people involved at all levels of the organization. Training and culture building will go a long way towards avoiding a problematic situation. Augmenting these two things with regular audits and with strict enforcement of policies in case of any violation help to make this issue manageable.

Ensuring that a country has laws to protect intellectual property and putting the best practices discussed above into effect reduces the chances of having to deal with intellectual property issues. But the threat cannot be eliminated in any place in the world, including the U.S.

FROM THE TRENCHES

In one case an employee was reported to have misappropriated sensitive information. Both the U.S. laws and the local laws of the offshore country were employed to deal with the situation. Remedies were sought both from the overseas company as well as from the individual responsible.

Establish processes for security and continuity

Events like 9/11 increases the need to assure that security issues are addressed and a formal contingency plan established and regularly updated. A contingency plan includes back-ups, use of secure vaults, and escrow arrangements when using a partner.

In order to develop an effective plan, managers should first understand the landscape.

For example, a facility located near New Delhi, India, which is the nation's capital and also closer to Kashmir (the scene of several conflicts between in India and Pakistan), has one level of risk. On the other hand, a facility located in Bangalore or Chennai, which is over one thousand miles from New Delhi, has a different level of risk.

In addition to the threat of war in the region(s), other possibilities should be assessed, such as:

♦ Natural disasters like floods.
♦ Local disturbances — whether the kidnapping of a politician, a strike, or the shutdown of cities for local causes.

A company should be prepared to deal with the following contingencies:

Human Resources	A bigger issue than the risk to physical systems, which can be backed up, are the human resources. If an offshore team is not available to handle its regular work, companies in the U.S. will have to find other personnel to maintain the offshore systems, handle their call centers, and staff their development projects.
Systems documentation	Engineering specifications, design docs, data sheets, ECOs, etc. play a key role in dealing with human resource contingencies. Up-to date engineering documentation provides other personnel with a reasonable chance to take over a project and sustain an effort during an emergency.

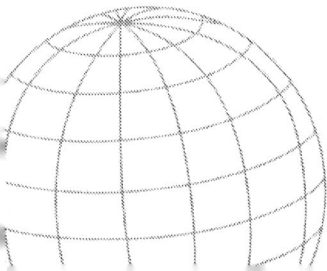

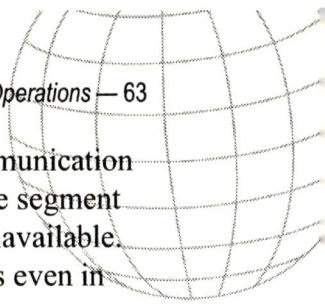

Communications	Many companies have redundant communication channels, which can be deployed if one segment in the communication link becomes unavailable. An organization may need this at times even in non-catastrophic situations.
Physical security of the site	Most companies control access to their facilities (whether their own or belonging to a partner). Companies should continually reassess their access control practices to determine whether they need to enhance the level of security depending on location and potential risks.
Travel Restrictions	The U.S. and other governments sometimes issue travel advisories. A project facing such a situation cannot count on team members being able to fly back and forth to conduct code reviews, deliver requirements, or review project status. One defense against it is remote communication technologies, such as videoconferencing.
Contracts	Companies need to know if their offshore partners can invoke *force majeure* in case of threat of war, which excuses a party from liability for contract obligations during that duration. Management must understand the precise nature of the exposure to be able to plan its own contingencies.

Account for variations in operating environment

Many infrastructure issues that are handled easily in the U.S. cannot be taken for granted elsewhere in the world, even though availability of infrastructure in many countries continues to improve. Failure to account for infrastructure difficulties can cause serious schedule delays.

A company doing offshore development must allow for the fact that some things might not work the same way in other countries as in the U.S. Researching offshore infrastructure issues requires an investment of resources, but making the investment provides for an increased degree of success. Some specifics worth checking include:

- Electric power (around the clock)
- Telephones
- Data lines
- Space
- Air conditioning
- Transferring equipment into and out of the country
- Availability of PC and Internet connection in homes
- Lead time for procuring the infrastructure

If the decision is made to work with a local partner, that company will address these issues. However, being aware of these differences will prevent surprises.

Establish customer relationships protocol

An offshore team that is responsible for support or for product maintenance and enhancement will probably come in contact with customers of the U.S. company. A clear-cut policy should be in place defining how the team should deal with these customers and identifying responsiveness requirements.

If properly managed, team members will not have to look to headquarters for approvals, as we mentioned before. In fact, response time requirements may deny team members sufficient time to come to headquarters for such approvals.

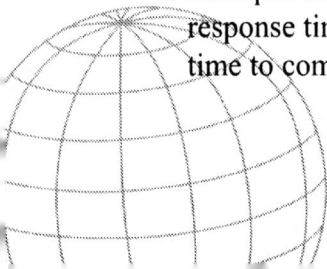

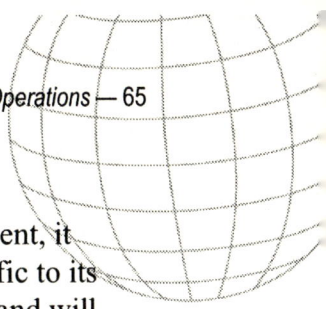

Create a best practices document

As a company gains experience with offshore development, it should develop its own operational level checklist specific to its environment. The checklist will be continually updated and will eventually evolve into an offshore template the organization can use. Typical topics in such a checklist will include the following:

♦ Whether the product has encryption that must be checked for export control compliance.
♦ Equipment needed by offshore organization.
♦ Skills needed by offshore organization.
♦ Specific plans for offshore development activities.

This is not a comprehensive list, but the bulleted items provide examples of the type of content that should be included in the checklist.

Establish and manage relationships

Successfully managing offshore development requires establishing relationships with several stakeholders. Relationships with strategic partners is the most obvious, but equally important are the relationships with the company's own employees and the public. Employee and public relations take on increased importance during economic downturns because of the fear of losing jobs to a foreign country.

Methods for addressing each segment are outlined below.

Partner relationships

Working with partners will succeed only when established upon mutually trusting relationships. Managing relationships with an offshore organization, therefore, should be viewed as much more than signing a contract with a vendor. The management task includes organizational commitment to continue building and sustaining the relationships.

Partner relationships should be pro-actively managed at all levels of the organization and goals should be clearly stated and well understood.

Factors that contribute to a successful relationship include:

Trust	Every partner transaction should be viewed as another step in building a mutually trusting relationship. Trust between parties is built over a period of time by delivering on commitments. But this is only half the effort. Trusting relationships are also facilitated by open communication between the parties. Trust is built when partners acknowledge and deal with failures as well as successes.
Common goals	Common goals are important to managing a relationship. In one example, the partner organization re-worked its internal compensation structure to achieve the shared goal of retaining significant knowledge in the partner organization.
Shared Knowledge	This involves not only the sharing of technical knowledge between partners, but providing access to each other's work environment and processes. In one example, technical personnel and technical leaders were expected to visit each other's facilities for a specified period of time each year in order to stay current in the other partner's changing environment.
Organizational linkage	To manage the relationships, the two organizations should be linked together at all levels. This includes information integration and process integration. In essence, one organization acts as an extension of the other, though the two are separate legal entities. Each company understanding the culture of the other makes the organizational linkage easier.

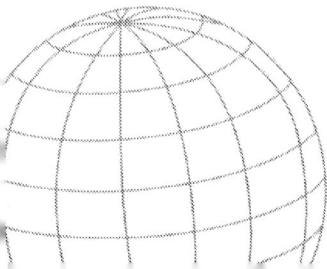

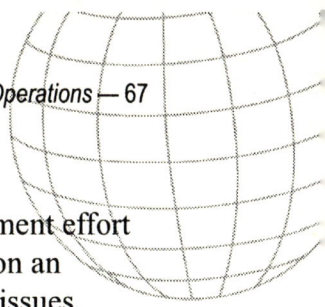

Employee relations

Employees have a major stake in how offshore development effort is handled. Management must communicate with them on an ongoing basis as to the offshore development goals and issues. They need to understand how the project might affect them.

Public relations

People in both countries are likely to be interested in the venture because of the potential for job losses and gains. The company must develop a policy to deal with the press on these issues. Depending on company philosophy and business requirements, the company may choose to be pro-active or reactive with the press.

CHAPTER SEVEN

Pay Attention to Culture

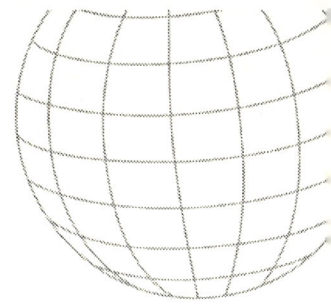

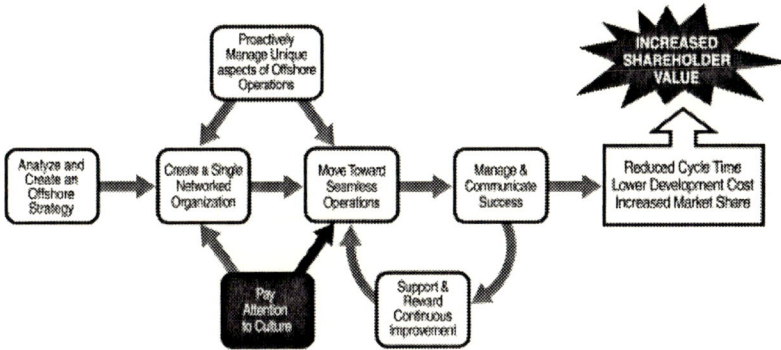

Every part of the world has culture unique to that area. These "social cultures" impact their "work cultures." For one thing, culture affects communications, which is much more than spoken words. Nonverbal communications such as greeting styles, gestures, facial expressions, and posture have definite culturally defined meanings. If managers do not understand the culture, it is easy to misinterpret behavior and intentions.

Culture provides the basis for self-identity, which includes the type of work one seeks. A certain type of work, such as testing, perhaps, might not be socially accepted and an organization will, therefore, have difficulty in attracting and retaining people for such work.

On the other hand, the same work culture might regard new product development as desirable and prestigious. An organization could use this as a carrot — parceling out development tasks with testing to create an environment of encouragement while still getting everything done that needs doing.

Most companies recognize that cultures around the world differ from one another. However, they often exert very little effort, if any, to identify specific cultural difference in an offshore development organization and to develop plans to deal with those differences.

The best companies take time to clearly define their own corporate and functional culture in terms of values, rituals, and behavior. The companies then identify how these cultural variations support, or fail to support, the corporate mission. They are prepared at that point to contrast and compare the local culture with any offshore cultural environment and to search for ways to leverage that particular culture to improve results.

Best practices

- ♦ Prepare to deal with language differences
- ♦ Address culturally defined issues
- ♦ Understand negotiation behavior and expectations
- ♦ Understand local culture

Prepare to deal with language differences

Language is more than simply words. Language gives structure to thought. A specific word does not mean exactly the same thing in any two cultures. A "yes" may not be a "yes" in the western sense of the word. For example, Japanese have a tendency for not wishing to offend. They are hesitant to voice disagreements, especially in a meeting. One has to read between the lines and extrapolate as much from what is left unsaid as from what is said.

Even when English is spoken, the local flavor of English can vary considerably. It is not uncommon for someone who speaks a British version of English to not fully comprehend the slang and idioms practiced in the U.S.

Words carry various meanings and values in other cultural contexts. For example, the common American word "contractor" is considered derogatory in some countries. The words "consultant" or "partner" are preferred.

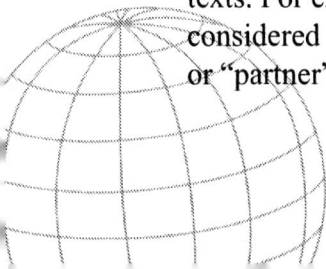

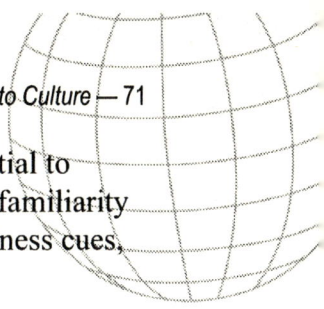

Skillful use of the language of the local country is essential to success in operating a business in that country. Without familiarity with the language, it is very difficult to be aware of business cues, negotiate, or understand and evaluate performance.

An organization needs explicit language policies for working in cross-cultural business environments.

Address culturally defined issues

Plan to address issues of context, time, information flow, and power in the offshore organization's own cultural milieu.

Every business operation is composed of innumerable activities ranging from hiring to workflow. These activities are only effective when the people involved understand the local, unspoken "ground rules" that govern communication, in general, and the sharing of information, in particular.

For example, the "old boys" network is the strongest channel for information flow at the top in high-context cultures. Context, time, information flow, and the power aspects of the local culture govern the operation of the "old boys" network to either promote or thwart the activities of the offshore enterprise.

If they are lucky, companies making minimal efforts to address multicultural needs get the same results as if they were using a homogenous team. At worst, the enterprise fails completely. Lack of understanding of multicultural issues tends to create frustration among team members, which consumes management time to resolve and leading to possibly disastrous results.

Companies must identify culturally appropriate communication technologies. Email and faxes are adequate for communication conducted between low-context cultures. However, high context cultures require voice and videoconferencing.

Here is some further information on how context, time, information flow, and power can affect offshore development efforts.

Context

The importance of context in communication varies with cultures. In high context cultures, verbal messages have little meaning without the associated context. Greater fluency in nonverbal behavior is required to successfully operate in high context cultures.

In eastern cultures, like China, people tend to rely on their history, status, and relationships in assigning a specific meaning to a communication event. However, in western cultures, people depend almost entirely on the specific verbal exchange.

Variation among cultures has implications for how companies function. The greater the variation among members of the team, the greater the communications challenge.

Time

Culture influences the way people value time. Americans tend to view time as a precious commodity and want to get down to business quickly. On the other hand, people from some other countries take a long time to get down to business. They want to get to know each other first.

These variations in orientation can become a source of frustration in cross-cultural teams. People from different cultures are likely to have difficulty adjusting to each other's style.

Information flow

Information flow consists of both the path and speed of communications. In a hierarchical culture, a lower-status worker would normally not question a superior. On the contrary, employees in the U.S. express their opinions more freely. Because of exposure to multinational companies attitudes are changing offshore, but care must be taken that hierarchy does not become an issue in a particular environment.

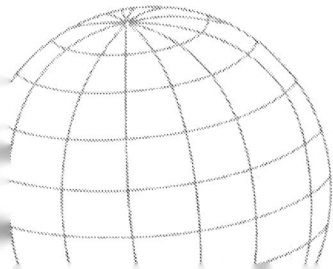

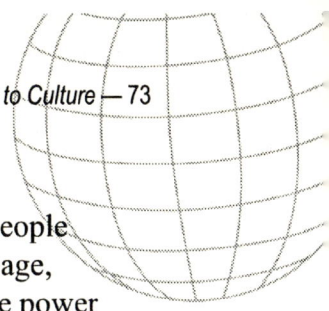

Power

Various degrees of power and equality are assigned to people within a particular group usually related to social class, age, wealth, education, race, and family. Cultures that ascribe power and equality on the basis of predetermined qualities such as family status or social classes have more rigid power structures and greater inviolable distance between social groups than cultures that award power on the basis of achievement.

Asian and Latin countries typically have more culturally ascribed power and less equality among groups than in the United States and Europe.

Understand negotiation behavior and expectations

Many companies take communication at face value based on their own culture and do not adjust to the local meanings in negotiation with offshore partners. This has a tendency to frustrate both parties.

Since negotiation processes differ radically from culture to culture, people working with offshore development projects need to understand the negotiating styles in a culture that is different from theirs. They must become aware of what one says and what one means, and the difference that might exist between those two.

A company must devise mechanisms to counteract variations in culture and understand what they are really negotiating. Otherwise, both parties in a negotiation will be unhappy when the time comes to deliver/receive the results of what the two apparently (but not really) agreed to.

A solution to the problem of cultural interference is to look for a middle way of negotiating rather than trying to impose one organization's cultural system on both parties. An effective way of doing this is to ask team members to design a workable team-based methodology of their own.

Understand local culture

A company that decides to operate in another country must become sensitive to local conditions in the offshore environment. Quite often the parent corporation is based in Western Culture such as Europe or the U.S., and the offshore location will be in a country such as India, China, or the Philippines.

Local management must understand the needs of the local organization and be able to effectively represent local needs at the corporate headquarters. If they lack credibility with the headquarters, morale at the local organization suffers, which is not in the best interests of the corporation.

In addition, local managers must be sensitive to the external environment in which they are operating. Local governments and businesses have certain operating policies and practices that are more easily managed when doing only development, as opposed to doing both development and marketing in the local country. The external environment takes on more importance when an organization plans to sell in the country. Sensitivity to local conditions has two advantages:

♦ Provides easier acceptance in the local community
♦ Provides a visible local face

These two things increase a company's ability to influence local policies that may influence how business is conducted there.

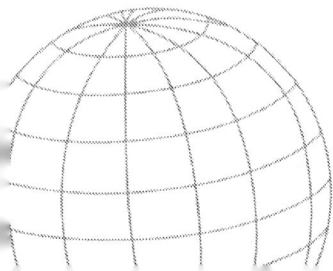

CHAPTER EIGHT

Manage and Communicate Success

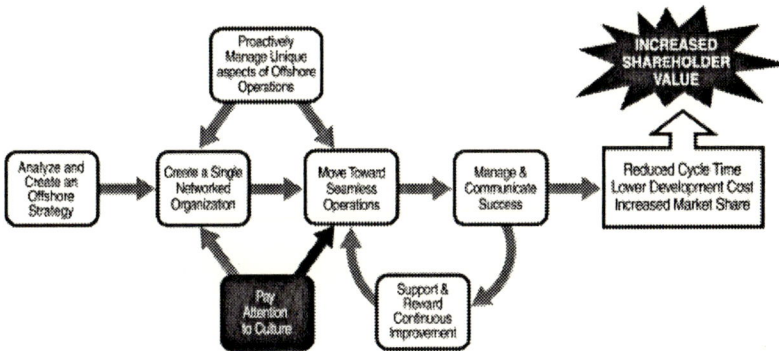

In any organization, there will be those who see the advantages of a new approach — in this case offshoring — and become supporters and early adopters. On the other hand, there are likely to be many who simply oppose change or specifically the offshoring approach. In order to demonstrate the viability of offshoring and build confidence, the offshoring team must focus on ensuring that the initial projects are outstandingly successful. In addition to initial confidence building, you need to establish a mechanism for ongoing communication of successes. Such communication takes on increased importance when the U.S. organization undergoes change, which is common to growing companies.

Best practices

- Manage a pattern of project successes
- Conduct multi-level marketing
- Communicate successes widely
- Become a pro-active change agent

Manage a pattern of project successes

"Nothing succeeds like success" is true in any effort, but this is especially relevant in offshore development. When embarking on the offshore effort, it is crucial that the first set of projects undertaken by the offshore organization be successful in order to build confidence at the U.S. headquarters. It is essential, therefore, to choose projects whose success can be demonstrated early in the life cycle of the offshore program.

Early visible success and a pattern of sustained successes do not happen by chance. Managers must consciously plan for it from the beginning. Here are some principles to help ensure success:

- ♦ Create "walk before you run" plans for implementing offshore development. To begin with, attempt a well-defined group of projects and concentrate all efforts on making them an astounding success.
- ♦ The philosophy of "Early visible success" should be well understood with everyone working towards that goal.
- ♦ Make the resulting success visible to the rest of the organization both offshore and at the headquarters, to instill confidence.
- ♦ Achieve a pattern of early visible successes. Then build the success of subsequent projects on the framework of the early successes. Selecting projects on identified criteria is one of the first key decisions that will lead to later successes.
- ♦ Create a portfolio with a representative cross section of outstandingly successful projects — large and small.
- ♦ Prototype new approaches before beginning implementation.

Prototyping is a great tool! The best organizations develop prototypes in order to increase chances of success, work out details, and then roll development out to the rest of the organization.

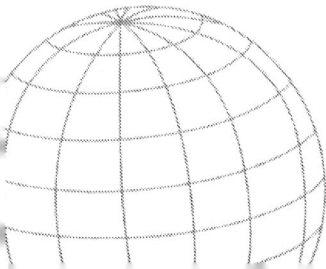

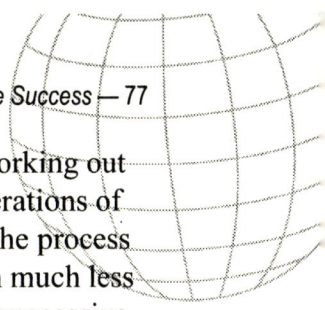

Taking an idea to the larger organization without first working out details, on the other hand, creates the risk of multiple iterations of debugging a single issue. Once a project is prototyped, the process can be replicated across the rest of the organization with much less risk, though customization may be necessary with each successive implementation.

In one highly successful implementation, the first year head count was deliberately held to 15 people. Only a limited number of projects with a high probability of success were chosen. Once these initial projects established the infrastructure and processes during the first year, scaling up was rapid and smooth.

FROM THE TRENCHES

Conduct multi-level marketing

To ensure the success of offshore development approach not only must the senior management of the parent company perceive that this is a good idea, but various levels of management (the depth depending on the size and structure of the organization) and individual contributors involved must be convinced that the project will succeed.

Here are some observations that can facilitate selling the idea:

♦ The organization conducts multi-level marketing to help the parent company (with its internal clients) understand the capabilities of the offshore organization competencies, which includes working with various levels of management as well as technical personnel.

♦ Instead of waiting as "order takers" to handle specific projects, the offshore organization engages in consultative selling. They aim to become both part of the parent strategy process and part of the budgeting process.

Communicate successes widely

Information about the success of the initial projects by the offshore organization must be disseminated so that other project managers gain confidence and become willing to focus on issues that pertain to their specific projects rather than focusing on the overall success of the program. The successes prove that the process is working and the challenge turns to replication. Issuing timely and factual communications to all users of the program builds acceptance for the offshore initiative and facilitates the generation of future projects.

The company should also communicate the successes to the offshore team that did the work to keep them motivated and to help them feel part of the team. For example, it should let the team members know that the project they worked on was deployed at AT&T and was wildly successful.

Become a pro-active change agent

In order to take maximum advantage of the offshoring approach, the company must engage in getting the approach accepted throughout the organization. This will require the offshore team becoming a pro-active change agent. People become agents of change by following four widely recognized steps:

- ♦ Create a vision that will be followed consistently in all activities.
- ♦ Clearly communicate and provide periodic reinforcement of the vision.
- ♦ Get everyone involved.
- ♦ Implement the vision.

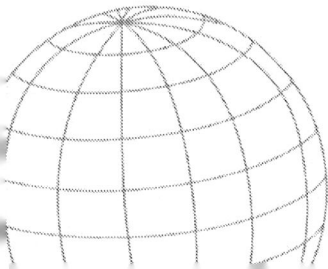

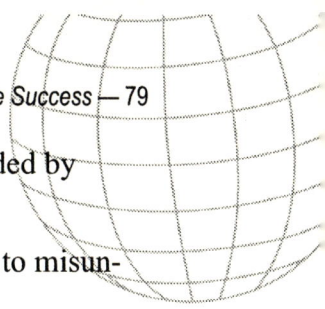

Before becoming a change agent, problems can be avoided by carefully going through the following simple checklist:

- ◆ Is it easy for a supporter of the proposed change to misunderstand the goal?
- ◆ Will the means to carry this out have to be invented or does the company already have prior experience?
- ◆ Is the opposition organized and do they have resources?
- ◆ Does this change threaten careers or empires?
- ◆ Is senior management sending conflicting signals?

If the answer to any of the above questions is "yes," the organization will have a difficult time managing the proposed change. Managers must address these issues before they can successfully make changes in their company.

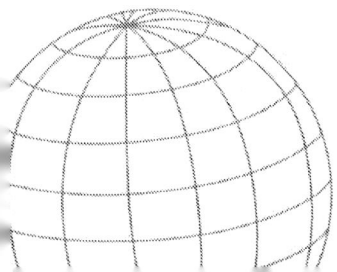

CHAPTER NINE

Pursue Continuos Improvement

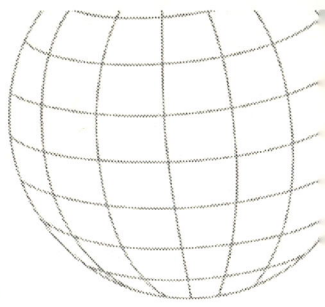

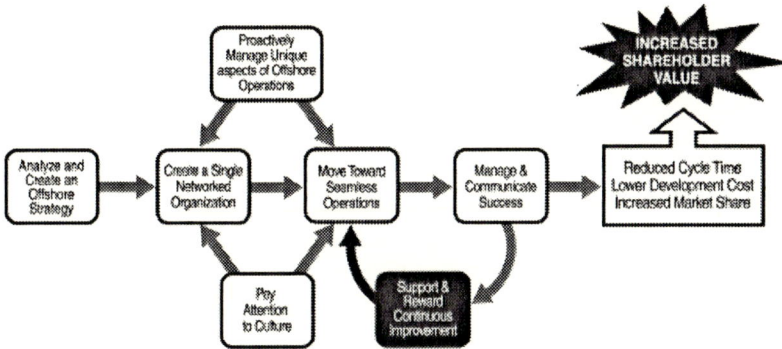

Adding a strong continuous improvement component to an off-shore development effort will ensure that rewards will not only last, but will increase over time.

Best practices

- ◆ Leverage time difference
- ◆ Move up the value chain

Leverage time difference

The offshore organization is often located in a different time zone, particularly when a U.S. based company sets up an operation in another country, such as India or China. Often, time differences cause difficulties in operations. However, this problem can be turned into a strategic advantage.

In one example, handling bug fixes to customers was distributed between the U.S. headquarters and its offshore organization. Data was passed between the two locations as each came on stream. Since the time difference was 12 hours, the total cycle time required to respond to a customer was often reduced by nearly 50%.

The same concept was extended in another case to distribute product development between U.S. and its offshore location; one location was responsible for code development and the other for testing. By employing a tag team approach, product development time was reduced, thereby giving this company a competitive advantage in bringing products to market faster.

This concept can be extended to leverage time differences around the world in providing technical support 24 hours a day by switching incoming customer calls to the appropriate center around the world. By setting up three centers, each in a different time zone and each coming online in eight-hour intervals, 24-hour coverage can be provided for customers. Such continuous customer support provides a strategic advantage.

To effectively implement these approaches, you must deploy the right processes for your environment along with tools for communication and collaboration.

Move up the value chain

While offshoring provides advantages of cost, access to skills and better processes, you can deploy these attributes in a variety of ways; in fact, how you deploy them will determine the value you will realize. In this context, you can think of offshoring in the same vain as platforms such as operating systems, data bases or processor chips. Each provides a certain set of capabilities and each company chooses to make use of these capabilities and build on them in their own unique way to create a different product.

Similarly, you can deploy capabilities provided by the offshore "platform," in many ways to create value — from plain cost reduction to competitive advantage. First, you need to understand where you currently are; then you can pursue an improvement initiative to move up the value chain.

The following offshoring maturity model along the lines of SEI CMM levels for software maturity, conceived and developed by Dr. Sridhar Mitta, a leading practitioner of offshoring, provides a good framework to embark on this effort.

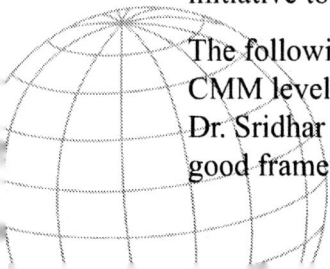

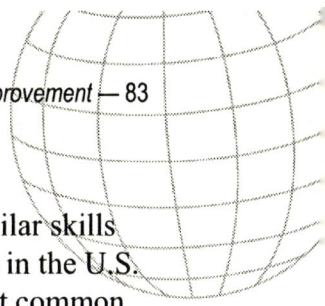

Level 1 — Wage arbitrage

At this level companies use offshore personnel with similar skills to execute the task in exactly the same way as was done in the U.S. The only difference is wage differential. This is the most common application of offshoring.

Impact: Cost reduction.

Level 2 — Better processes and people with higher qualification

Many offshore companies have invested heavily in process improvements and process certifications such as ISO 9000, Six Sigma and SEI CMM Level 5. Given the combination of better processes and cost advantage, you may be able to use offshoring for improving your own processes. Offshore call centers are usually staffed by more qualified personnel than in the west — college graduates instead of high school graduates.

Impact: Quality improvement; cost reduction.

Level 3 — Introduce products/services that would not have "made the cut."

In most companies, demands from marketing for products exceed available engineering resources. Product plans are developed to identify what the company will be able to undertake during the next period (usually a year). Key considerations for inclusion in the product plan are market size, cost and availability of resources. Offshoring can help you expand product plans — you may be able to include additional products because of their lower cost of development. This will enable you to better serve existing markets and/or serve smaller markets that you would not have been able to.

Packaged software provides generic solutions to serve the needs of a large number of companies. For example ERP packages are designed this way. Some companies have business processes that do not fit nicely into the models assumed by the ERP packages. One answer is customization, which can be expensive. However, in certain cases, the level of customization and the corresponding cost can be prohibitive. Offshoring may provide an alternative strategy where a custom solution can be built from the ground up — one that meets 100% of the needs at an affordable cost.

Impact: Increased revenue

A multi-billion dollar computer company and a leader in the fault tolerant market offered products on its proprietary operating system. However, the market demand to offer its products on an industry-standard operating system became apparent, though the market was smaller. The company could not meet this demand and also maintain and support the current platform with its existing resources. By utilizing an offshore partner, the company was able to address this need thereby expanding its market and consequently revenues.

FROM THE TRENCHES

Level 4 — Strategic advantage:

Unique and innovative ways of combining approaches described in levels 1, 2 and 3 can provide you strategic advantage. You can employ different business models to provide more leverage than just the cost advantage. You can leverage marketing know how unique to the region (in addition to offshore technical skills) to create products explicitly for the region. Other examples that follow illustrate this point further.

Impact: Increased revenue

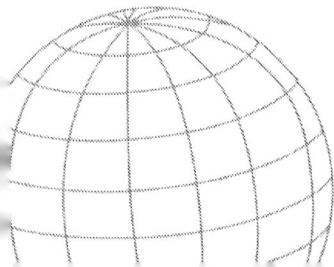

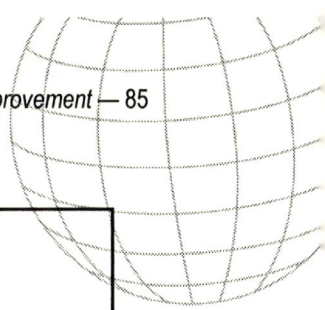

Innovative use of offshoring helped a computer company survive a delay in meeting market needs. When this company began developing its next generation products, forecasts showed that the cycle would take 2 years and will consume its entire internal resources. The management recognized that two years without new products would spell disaster. Rather than wait for two years, the company decided to use its offshore partner to develop an interim product and bring it to market within 1 year; the rationale to go offshore was not just lower cost, but the ability to free internal resources to focus on the next generation products and to at least meet some of the key market requirements quicker. As events unfolded, a delay from the company's chip vendor nearly knocked the company out of business — with this delay the new product could not be shipped for three years instead of two. The interim products developed in partnership with the offshore vendor met enough market needs for the company to keep going, till the full product line became available.

GE offshored its credit card processing application; the immediate effect was reduction of cost by 25%; six sigma processes were then applied to this operation resulting in another 20% cost reduction. A further step was to customize the image processing yielding a further reduction of 30%. These moves, taken in combination, are estimated to have reduced their cost by about 75%.

GE appliances in India started a new activity for pricing of their washers and other appliances. This utilizes nearly 100 Ph.Ds. in statistics who build and run the models. This could not have been done in the west, easily — it is hard to assemble such a staff since they may not be available; even if it could have been done, it would have been too expensive to justify.

A majority of the companies operate in the first 2 levels; they have ample opportunity to move up the value chain.

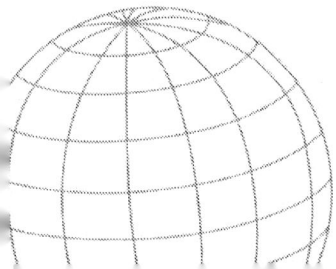

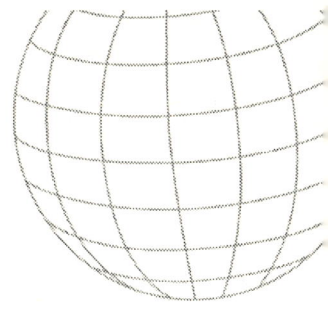

CHAPTER TEN

Offshore Technical Support

This chapter is devoted to topics specific to offshore technical support and should be read in conjunction with material presented earlier in the book. In addition to availability of talent at competitive prices, other recent trends such as significant drop in telecom costs, technology and tools for remote management have driven the proliferation of offshore contact centers in many countries. Activities these centers address include inbound calls, outbound calls, live chat, email responses, sales support, customer support and technical support. Here are selected events that indicate a strong trend towards offshoring in these areas:

♦ Microsoft works with 198 contact centers across the globe; has 5 vendors in India who provide voice-based support and is reported to be considering increasing the volume of voice-based support from India. Its contact centers offer tele-sales, operational support that ranges from mundane questions concerning software to technical support for complex queries.

♦ Baan, one of the manufacturing sector's biggest software makers is developing India into a major R&D and technical support hub. Located in Hyderabad, its contact center operations provide technical support to global clients. In addition, this center houses nearly half the R&D staff for the company. Baan has taken this step after having had a smaller presence in Bombay for several years.

♦ Hughes Software Systems is expanding its back-office business unit by hiring more people and extending the range of services offered. This unit provides online customer care services using voice, chat and e-mail across multiple industry segments like IT, networking, telecom, automotive, insurance, banking and financial services. The back-office unit initially began with technical support to its parent company's Direcway service, which provides high-speed Internet access via satellite to more than 160,000 subscribers.

♦ Dell established contact center operations in Bangalore to provide a variety of support functions including technical support. The staff grew rapidly from a few hundred to currently estimated size of about 3000. This has helped the company keep down the cost of providing round-the-clock support.

In late 2003, Dell decided to relocate their technical support for business customers back to the U.S. It is reported that the issues were heavy accents and scripted responses. However, Dell continues to provide consumer and other support functions from its offshore center and maintains its large presence.

♦ Lehman Brothers began using two Indian firms TCS and Wipro to manage several of its information technology operations. In late 2003, Lehman stopped outsourcing its IT help desk, which handles employee reports of computer problems. Specific reasons for the decision are not made public. However, Lehman continues to use India for a variety of other functions and in fact is reported to be boosting its use of India.

♦ Tokyo based Trend Micro, a leading company in antivirus applications provides technical support from its center in Mumbai.

♦ Even venture capital companies are getting into the act. Silicon Valley venture capital firm Sequoia Capital led a $22 million investment into Indian contact-center firm 24/7 Customer. Sequoia is famous for backing technology giants like Yahoo, Oracle, Cisco Systems and Google. "Sequoia does not generally invest in service companies; but makes exceptions when the market is large and lends itself to automation, 24/7 is at the beginning of a trend of Indian service companies catering to large corporations, especially in the United States", according to published reports.

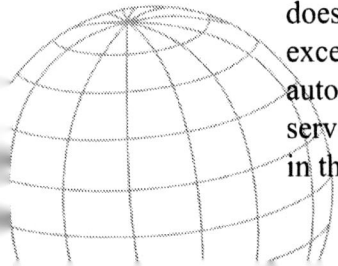

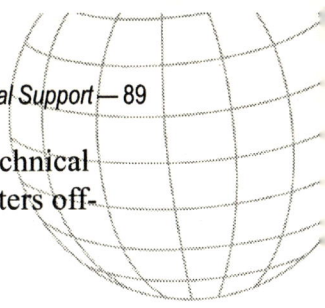

In addition, companies of various sizes in a variety of technical disciplines have either established technical support centers offshore or reported to be considering such a move.

Definitions

For terminology used in this chapter the context/definitions are provided here. To define the support process, it helps to define the goals of each support tier in the organization and their roles and responsibilities. The following tables provide example of Responsibility Hierarchy and Tiered Support.

Support Tier	Responsibility	Goals
Tier 1 Support	Full-time help desk support Answer support calls, open and manage trouble tickets, work on problem resolution up to 15 minutes, document ticket and escalate to appropriate tier 2 support	Resolution of 40% of incoming calls
Tier 2 Support	Queue monitoring, network management, station monitoring Place trouble tickets for software identified problems Implement Take calls from tier 1, vendor, and tier 3 escalation Assume ownership of call until resolution	Resolution of 100% of calls at tier 2 level
Tier 3 Support	Must provide immediate support to tier 2 for all priority 1 problems Agree to help with all problems unsolved by tier 2 within SLA resolution period	No direct problem ownership

Source: Cisco white paper

Service Level Definitions

This table shows example of problem severity for an organization.

Severity 1	Severity 2	Severity 3	Severity 4
Severe business impact LAN user or server segment down Critical WAN site down	High business impact through loss or degradation, possible workaround in place Campus LAN down; 5-99 users affected Domestic WAN site down International WAN site down Critical performance impact	Some specific network functionality is lost or degraded, such as loss of redundancy Campus LAN performance impacted LAN redundancy lost	A functional query or fault that has no business impact for the organization

Source: Cisco white paper

How offshore centers handle calls

Offshore support centers utilize telecommunication and computer technologies to automate various inbound and outbound telephone and web based activities. Most common media are:

- ◆ Telephone
- ◆ E-mail
- ◆ Web chat
- ◆ Collaborative browsing
- ◆ Web/self-service
- ◆ Instant Messaging

Offshore vendors usually have a connecting point in the U.S. Once you connect to that facility (and you may need to incur the cost of such connection), they usually have the infrastructure in place to process calls from that point forward.

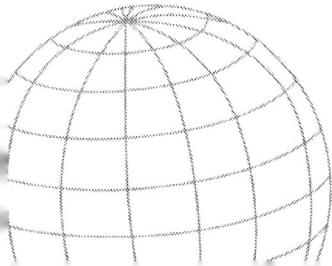

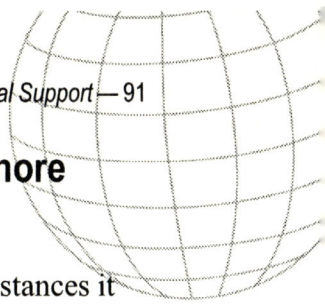

What types of projects qualify for offshore technical support?

You can consider offshoring tiers 1, 2 and 3. In some instances it may be easier to do one or the other tier offshore, because of your unique circumstances. Many product categories can be considered. Here are some examples:

- Software products
  Examples: Oracle Data Base, MS Exchange, MS Word
- Networking products
  Example: Routers
- Enterprise applications
  Examples: PeopleSoft, Oracle, Baan
- Web site support
- Desk top and personal computer support
- Data center management and operations

Collaboration tools

Recent advances in technology have provided Internet-based tools that enable collaboration and reduce the feeling of separation. Virtually everything a technical support person could do in a face-to-face meeting can be done on a remote basis. For example, "Support Center" from Webex offers the following capabilities:

- View, diagnose and solve problems online
- Run applications to ensure proper installation and configuration
- Include other technical support personnel, customers, or experts, with the touch of a button
- Download patches or updates to the customer's computer
- Upload customer files for analysis
- Showcase products and features with two-way view/share
- Record the entire support session for archival and training purposes
- Deliver management reports and session logs
- Live video can be streamed to personalize support sessions

Source: Webex (www.webex.com)

Tools from Linktivity allows your desktop to:

- Communicate via keyboard chat or real-time voice chat
- Direct a remote customer to a Web site using co-browse features
- Conduct a remote control session and operate a remote customer's PC
- Perform remote systems diagnostics
- Restore a remote user's PC to a previously working configuration
- Transfer files
- Remotely install and configure software
- Remotely configure (or re-configure) system settings

Source: Linktivity (**www.linktivity.com**)

In addition, Instant Messaging is widely used for collaboration. Such tools enable you to not only locate support personnel anywhere, they also allow you to conduct remote training – reducing your travel and related costs.

Best practices unique to technical support

Maintaining quality

In addition to the best practices articulated earlier in the book, you should consider the following steps:

1. Hire the right agents: Get involved in agent acquisition. Use testing mechanisms to determine the suitability of a prospective employee. Since these tests can be administered via the web in multiple languages, you can conduct first level screening from your own location in the U.S.

2. Monitor performance, individually and up the organization chain. Set up programs to score each agent, their supervisor and eventually the whole offshore organization. This monitoring can be performed live, real time, or in an offline fashion. There are tools available such as Witness

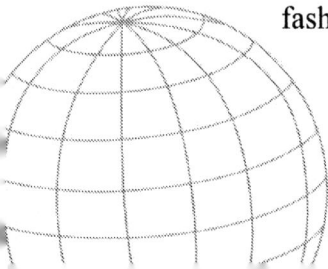

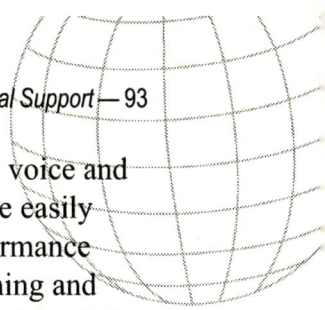

(www.witness.com) that allow recording of both voice and data of a customer interaction. These files can be easily reviewed and monitored for compliance to performance goals and standards. You can conduct live coaching and live assessments. Whether you use live, offline or blended monitoring, set up regular (for example monthly) review/ feed back to help the organization improve and grow. It is imperative that this process be established and maintained. This is not a component of the service model that can be delegated if the organization outsourcing its customer interactions wants to maintain a high level of customer acceptance and satisfaction.

3. Establish quality feed back systems with metrics: Compare performance metrics with the industry and with customer satisfaction surveys. You can track performance of the individuals and the specific organizational units.

There are several tools that do this; AON Consulting is one of the leaders in this field — www.aoncons.com

Agent training in accents and culture

The offshore service providers usually go to great lengths to train their agents in western accents and culture. Some of the practices used:

- ◆ Beginning with the initial interview, checking communication skills
- ◆ Training recruits in pronouncing specific words
- ◆ Staying abreast of current events by watching news broadcasts like CNN, NBC and watching western TV programs to pickup cultural aspects

Staffing issues

Technical support personnel need to understand both the technology aspects and people aspects, since they will deal directly with customers. Your selection process needs to take this into account.

Time difference — pros and cons

One of the advantages of offshore support is the ability to use follow the sun model so that the offshore facility can provide support in their "normal" hours for "outside normal" hours in the west. However, if you use the offshore facility for support during normal times in the west, then they need to work in their night hours; this can lead to turnover of personnel.

Business Processes

Make sure that the business processes are robust, clearly articulated and understood by everyone concerned.

> Real time nature: Unlike development projects, technical support is mostly a real time activity (levels 1 and 2).

> Customer facing: Since the contact center personnel will deal directly with customers, they are constantly representing you to your customers.

Extension of your own operation

If you outsource, after a period of time it is easy to fall into the trap "out of sight out of mind"; it may not be adequate to do periodic reviews; you need to manage it as if it is your own operation – but in a different location.

Build on successes: Because of the criticality of the impact on operations, try a pilot, make sure that the processes work and then ramp up.

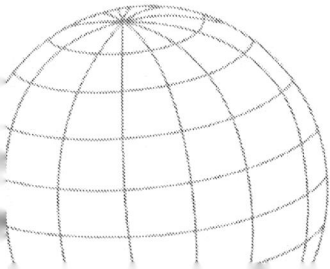

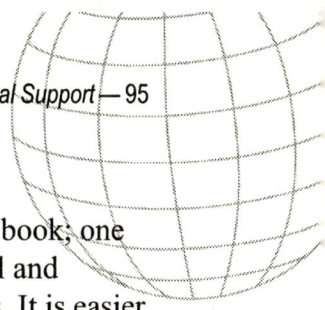

Project selection — Contextual knowledge

Project selection criteria has been covered earlier in the book; one key aspect worth emphasizing — the issue of contextual and cultural knowledge that the offshore entity must possess. It is easier to transfer technical information to an offshore entity. However, when one needs to go beyond scripts, technical information and into the realms of intuitive/cultural issues, it is much harder to train the offshore entity; for example, just being polite and reading from the script is inadequate if the customers' need is very time sensitive; escalation to the next level or bringing someone else into a call that is not going well (from the customer perspective) requires the staff to make judgment call in real time — at the end the objective is to assure that the customer is not only given the right technical solution, but is clearly satisfied with the experience.

Ongoing reviews

In order to make sure that your operation is meeting the goals and staying current with industry, you should institute regular reviews — once a quarter is the frequency most commonly used.

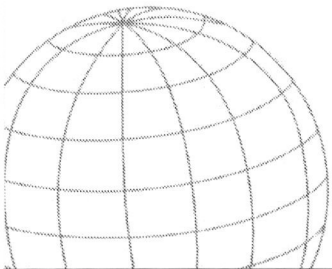

CHAPTER ELEVEN

Case Studies

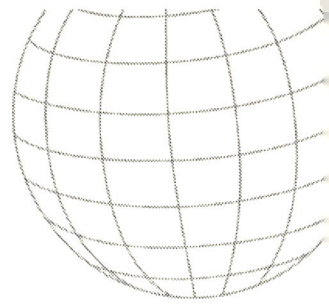

We will now look at case studies showing both successes and failures, since lessons can be learned from both. We will withhold names from the second category because of its sensitive nature. However, our information is from reliable sources.

Success: HP — Nonstop Enterprise Division (NED)

History and Background

The Nonstop Enterprise Division (NED) is part of HP, which was originally Tandem Computers. Compaq acquired Tandem in the mid 90s. Compaq, in turn, became part of HP in 2002.

NED's effort to leverage offshore resources began in the early 1990s while Tandem was still an independent company with sales of $2 billion and an engineering staff of about 2,500 in four divisions.

Tandem's offshore project was one of the pioneering efforts at developing and maintaining software products using the offshore model. Of particular interest is the fact that Tandem's computers run mission critical applications. Therefore, the company needed to assure that the quality of software developed continued to meet its high standards, regardless of where it was developed. So the issues of distance, visibility, and control were of significant concern as the company embarked on applying the offshore development model.

The rest of this section provides a view of best practices that made it a successful venture. Major best practices were:

♦ Establishing a clear mission statement
♦ Developing a strategy to partner rather than to build
♦ Selecting the right partners
♦ Creating a pilot to ensure success before ramping up
♦ Treating partners as extensions of the headquarters engineering

Mission Statement

Recognizing that the offshore development initiative was of major importance to the company, senior management set the direction to leverage talent available globally in order to:

♦ Lower engineering cost structure
♦ Free U.S. personnel for higher-value projects

The mission statement provided a clear focus to the initiative and greatly expedited decision making. In addition, senior management was committed to the initiative from its inception.

Build vs. partner

The company considered several countries, sent a team of executives to those that made the short list, and finally settled on India — though India's capabilities for software development were not well known in the early 90s.

In addition to cost, key considerations included availability of engineering talent, in particular those with experience in system software, and the ability to ramp up quickly.

Instead of choosing to build its own operations, which would have required a longer time frame because of the infrastructure existing at the time, the company chose to partner with two companies — Wipro and TCS.

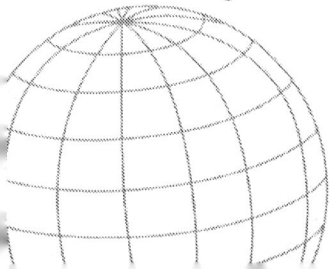

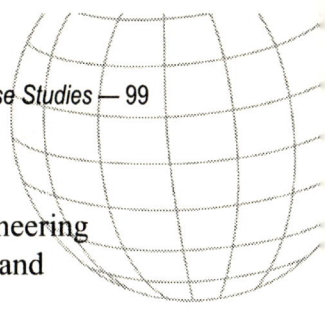

Create pilot, assure success, and ramp up

The offshore development initiative began with 15 engineering personnel working on four projects. Both the personnel and projects were carefully chosen.

During the "technology transfer" phase, NED invested heavily in training partner personnel because of the proprietary and complex nature of the technologies involved. The training included classroom instruction and hands-on training followed by working side-by-side with their U.S. counterparts to do actual development.

Once the engineers were successful in carrying out tasks on their own, they moved back to their own organizations in India and began executing tasks remotely.

After moving to India, the fact that the team members had established personal relationships with their U.S. counterparts was of huge value in resolving issues that came up.

The goal of everyone involved during this phase was "early visible success." The teams resolved other technical issues as they came up and met all the milestones and quality goals, thereby establishing a solid foundation and a successful prototype.

At this stage, the offshore development initiative began ramping up by taking on other projects from across the company.

Some of the key best practices at this phase of the initiative:

♦ Training the trainer: Because of the technologies involved, new engineers had to acquire knowledge specific to NED. Rather than having NED train all new personnel, some training responsibility was transferred to partner organizations. In essence NED trained trainers who, in turn, trained new entrants to the initiative. The training the trainer approach helped to better manage the training investment and at the same time reduced the cycle time required to train new personnel. Partners could now conduct training on their own, at their convenience, and without having to wait for someone from the U.S. to make a trip to India.

♦ Pipelining: Since the offshore development initiative was ramping up, the partner personnel needed to assure a continuous supply of talent. NED shared the scaling plans with partners and they were able to recruit and put into place personnel who were ready to take on specific projects as they became available. This turned out to be a win-win situation for both parties.

♦ Setting up infrastructure: Because of the specialized nature of the technology, it became essential for NED to set up a development lab at a partner location overseas. This meant significant up-front planning and logistics for setting up the lab and a network to integrate them into the U.S. operations.

♦ Maintaining quality: Since the pilot project established clear processes, scaling and maintaining quality was easier.

Types of projects

NED offshore projects eventually spanned software development, sustaining, quality assurance, and information systems. As confidence in the approach began to increase, more complex projects were sent offshore.

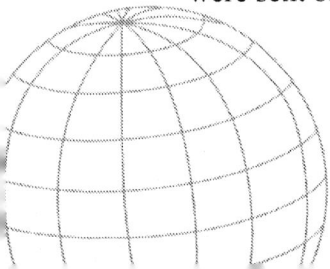

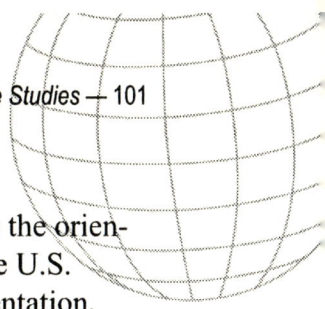

Partners as extension of NED

One key to NED's success in offshore development was the orientation of the overseas organization as an extension of the U.S. headquarters engineering team. The combination of orientation, attitude, and actions that followed out of this global team approach was based on that premise.

Here are two examples of how this orientation was implemented:

♦ Communications were possible and encouraged across all levels of the organization — from developers to executives. A partner developer physically located half way around the world had the ability to communicate with his counterparts just the same as with a NED developer in another building, except that he could not physically meet with the developer. The offshore developer was considered a full-fledged member of the global engineering team.

♦ Partners were made aware of upcoming needs and could manage infrastructure and staffing accordingly.

Results

♦ Cost savings contributed 10% of Earnings Per Share (EPS) in 1995 for Tandem.
♦ The organization gained additional capacity through the creation of a location-independent, networked organization.
♦ New products were introduced that could not have been done by utilizing local engineering staff, because of the price point.

Key reasons for success

- ◆ Recognition from top management about the strategic importance and consequent support.
- ◆ Willingness to invest at the appropriate levels from the first day.
- ◆ Heavy emphasis on establishing and managing relationship with partners and stakeholders throughout the company at all levels.
- ◆ Well-thought-out road map. For example, during the first year, the size of operation was limited to 15 developers and the required infrastructure was put in place. It was scaled up to 100 people in year two and more the following year.
- ◆ Emphasis on "Early visible success." Initial projects were carefully chosen and intensely managed to assure outstanding success. This made it easier to promote the offshoring approach throughout the company.
- ◆ Retention of "ownership" of the products by the respective line organizations.
- ◆ Selection of partners that not only met the technical requirements, but the "cultural" requirements, as well. For example, one partner had prior experience with operating systems and in dealing with "systems level" products.

Success: General Electric (GE)

GE is one of the large users of talent from India. Currently GE utilizes an estimated 6,000 people in software. While precise numbers are hard to come by, one estimate is that GE realizes savings of about $240 million annually through India-based offshore software development, which of course flows directly to the bottom line.

In the rest of this section, we present how GE has gone about establishing and managing these operations.

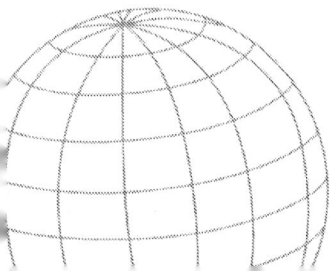

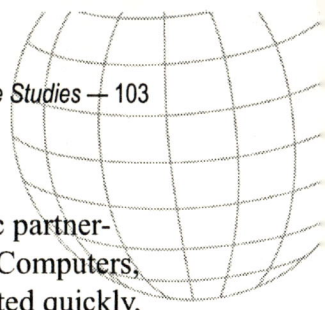

Organizational Model

GE began outsourcing to India in 1992 through strategic partnerships with four major companies — TCS, Wipro, Patni Computers, and Infosys. Outsourcing gave GE the ability to get started quickly, since they did not have to deal with local issues and infrastructure, as well as receiving the benefits that come from outsourcing to an existing organization. Multiple organizations also meant that they could leverage unique strengths of each organization in addition to creating competition.

The mix of partners has changed since 1992 with Infosys and Wipro exiting the fold and Satyam and Mascott entering. By 2001 GE had a headcount of about 6,000 professionals in partner organizations.

In addition, GE has established its own operations to tap into the Indian talent pool. The operations range from The Jack Welch Research Center at Bangalore, staffed by Ph.D.'s, to a call center staffed by several thousand personnel in GE's center in Hyderabad.

The 70-70-70 Strategy

GE established a corporate strategy to move projects offshore. Managers are targeted to outsource 70% of their efforts. Out of that, 70% is intended for preferred vendors. From what goes to preferred vendors, 70% needs to be offshore.

Given this strategic direction, operating managers are more inclined to use offshore resources. In addition, senior management takes keen interest to assure that this strategy is implemented. Different divisions have implemented this strategy at different levels; however there is no issue about whether or not to use offshore resources. In this respect, GE is way ahead of many other companies that are still trying to come to grips with the notion of leveraging offshore resources.

Partners as extension of the global organization

GE has successfully implemented the notion of treating partners as extensions of the global organization. For example, GE has been open about sharing their strategies with its partners, which includes planned use of offshore resources. Armed with this information, the partners are better equipped to develop their own internal plans for ramping up.

Once a year GE invites partners for an offsite feedback session in retreats like Katmandu. At these sessions both partners and GE openly share what is right with the programs and what needs fixing. This open dialogue has helped both GE and their partners move forward together.

In the interest of mutual success, GE line mangers are innovative in implementing corporate policies. For example, a purchasing agreement called for payments at a particular rate. Everyone recognized that the mandated rate was not adequate to attract and retain the best talent. The managers, therefore, worked out a "blended rate" for on-shore and offshore payments. By doing this, GE complied with corporate guidelines, while providing enough leeway for the partner to attract and retain the best talent. This spirit of cooperation promotes success.

When new technologies like Broad Vision came on the scene, GE recognized that their Indian partners did not have the people with the required skills so they used their corporate buying power to get companies like Broad Vision to train partner engineers. This turned out to be a win-win strategy because GE was able to realize significant cost benefits over comparable U.S. costs while the partners were able to gain expertise in new technology areas.

Partner management

GE managers take active part in managing relationships with offshore teams. Managers travel to partner sites, as necessary. Rigorous quarterly reviews attended by business unit managers in addition to technical managers, are a part of the overall program.

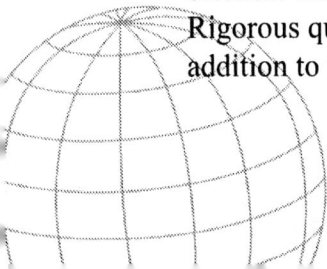

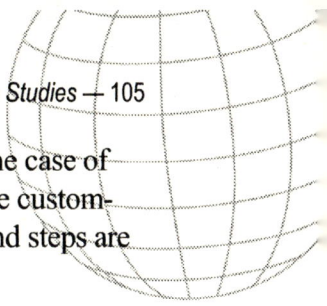

Customer satisfaction surveys are conducted annually. In the case of Information systems, users of these systems are the ultimate customers. Feedback from these surveys is considered seriously and steps are taken to make indicated modifications to the program.

Partner personnel were invited to take part in GE's six sigma training programs, thereby extending the core values of the company to partner organizations.

Knowledge retention

GE recognizes the need to retain knowledge and experience in critical areas. Programs are established to identify core personnel, reward them with appreciation programs such as a night out, lunches, dinners, and other incentives.

Types of Projects

GE has outsourced a wide variety of projects. The initial projects focused on maintenance of legacy IBM mainframe systems. The projects progressed into client server development projects, Y2K projects, web enabling projects, e–commerce projects, and Oracle package implementation.

GE established the Jack Welch Research Center in Bangalore, where scientists perform statistical analysis in specialized areas. In their own call centers, GE provides customer service and support for a variety of functions across the company.

Scaling strategy

GE has a very clear scaling strategy. During the initial phase, they outsourced clearly definable projects with the size of projects increasing as confidence increased. For instance, the initial size was in the range of $100K which gradually progressed to $2M.

The process of offshore development is also guided step-by-step. The first set or projects are executed side by side with their U.S. counterparts, but staffed by partner engineers. When sufficient technology transfer and confidence building occurs, the team transfers to a nearby location, but is allowed to manage on its own.

Once this step is successful, the team is transferred offshore to an Overseas Development Center (ODC). Once the team executes successfully from an ODC, the size of the team is increased.

One of the key reasons for success in this model is assuring that proper transfer of the processes and culture takes place in an orderly fashion so that scaling occurs gradually with confidence building at each step for both parties.

Success: Agile Software

Background

Agile Software was founded in 1995. As the leader in Product Chain Management, it delivers solutions that enable companies to work with their customers and suppliers to efficiently build better, more profitable products faster, and at less cost.

The Agile Product Chain Management solution is comprised of Product Collaboration, Product Sourcing, and Product Service and Improvement. These business-ready application suites allow seamless communication and collaboration across an entire supply chain — spanning design, sourcing, building, sales, and service.

Agile's enterprise-class solutions are built upon a world-class architecture that is robust, highly scalable, and secure. The four-tier, standards-based architecture leverages XML and EAI technologies to manage Product Chain DNA information across all Agile solutions. Built with standards-based APIs, the entire suite is business-ready, yet highly customizable.

Agile has over 750 customers, including GE Medical, International Paper, Juniper Networks, Lucent, HP, Dell Computer, Flextronics International, NVIDIA, Philips, Sycamore Networks, Texas Instruments, and Zhone Technologies.

Agile began the initiative to leverage offshore resources in early 2002.

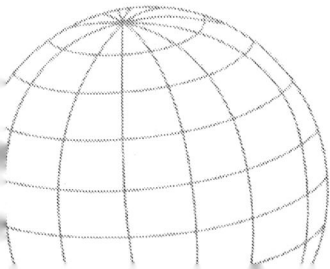

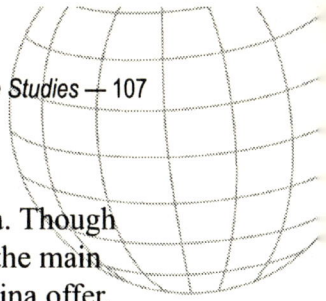

Strategy and Organization

Agile has set up development centers in India and China. Though San Jose, California is clearly the integration point and the main center, Agile leverages the advantages that India and China offer. For example localization for the Asian market is carried out at their China center. Rather than go the route of partners, Agile decided to set up its own operations abroad.

Fast Start

The center in India was launched in a span of 90 days following the final go ahead, with an initial staff of 20 and is delivering products from the offshore location.

Major reasons for Agile's success include:

- ◆ Clear strategy and Road Map.
- ◆ Ready acceptance.
- ◆ Seeding operations with existing employees.

Prior to launching, Agile developed a clear strategy and detailed road map that addressed:

- ◆ Goal identification and definition.
- ◆ Specific evaluation of environment and work content to determine offshore suitability.
- ◆ How to organize it; impact on internal resources.
- ◆ Projects for year 1 and forecasts for 3 years.
- ◆ Business impact analysis.
  - ◆ Investments and start up costs.
  - ◆ Multi year cost saving analysis and ROI.
- ◆ Risk Analysis and mitigation strategy.
- ◆ Transfer of information.
- ◆ Key milestones.

In order to expedite the process and enhance confidence in the offshore strategy, Agile sought independent external advisors to develop and implement an offshore development approach.

While the notion of offshore development can require convincing the development staff, Agile is fortunate to have a large number of personnel who readily saw the advantages to the company.

As is true of many Silicon Valley companies, Agile has several engineers of Indian and Chinese origin. Many of them were willing to return to their homelands and continue to be part of Agile. Because of this, the company was able to transfer several key employees to India and China to serve as the startup team for operations in that country. Due to this approach, going offshore meant that, initially the same people who were working in San Jose, now are working in either India or China. Since issues of transfer of technology, culture, and processes are eliminated, a rapid start with high confidence has been possible.

With both the India and China centers already delivering early stage results, Agile is on the way to successfully scaling up their operations.

Failure: Outsourced project from a startup

This example is drawn from an attempt to do offshore work by a startup in Silicon Valley. The project failed to meet expectations.

From the beginning the project was set up to be short-term (which proved to be a mistake). The approach was "Find a vendor, throw it over the wall."

Three months into the project, management was surprised to learn that they could not transfer a license for tools to a vendor in a timely fashion, in order to develop the product. In an effort to meet product release deadlines, managers decided to pull it back and complete it locally at much higher costs than if it were done here from the beginning.

This incident offers lessons in how not to do offshore development. Key among the project deficiencies were:

- ◆ Lack of planning.
- ◆ Inadequate investment in partnering and project management.
- ◆ Making cost the only driver; hence not enough attention or investment made in success.

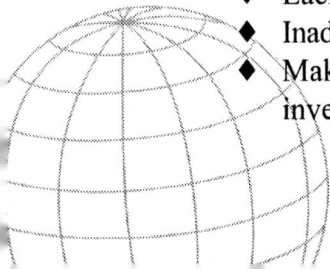

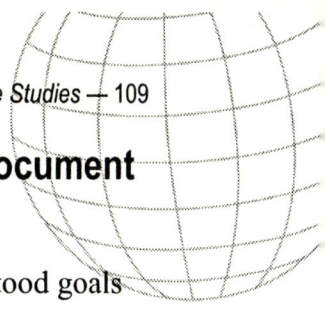

Failure: Outsourced project from a large document management company

Selecting the right projects together with clearly understood goals are very important to a successful effort.

This company chose to work with a leading vendor offshore in the field of high-speed printing. At the time, this was new technology and goals were not defined. As the effort progressed, no visible progress occurred. Engineering management, closer to the project, understood the vague nature of the work and realized the reasons for the perceived lack of progress.

However, the senior management decided to cancel the project since they could not see progress. In hindsight, better expectation management inside the company may have saved this project.

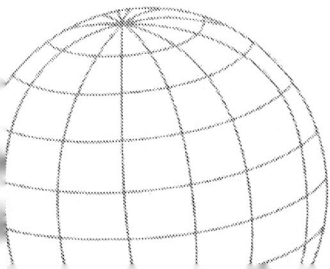

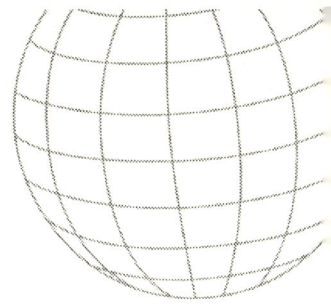

CHAPTER TWELVE

Steps in Implementing

While the whole arena of offshore development requires many different activities, the first step is to secure top-level management commitment and communicate that to the organization. In addition, you should establish a champion for your company and have that person report to a senior executive.

Subsequent to that, the following list of tasks should be addressed. This is not a checklist of each and every task to undertake, but includes the most important ones.

1. Develop road map

- Establish success criteria
- Choose a country
- Select entry strategies for the country
  - Outsourcing
  - Joint venture
  - Subsidiary
  - Build-Operate-Transfer (BOT)
- Set up project selection criteria
- Select projects for Phase One and determine ramp rate for three years
- Determine infrastructure
- Establish major milestones
- Develop financials
  - Total cost
  - Savings
  - Investment

2. Establish offshore capacity

If your company chooses to partner:

♦ Create RFP and target candidates
♦ Review responses and develop short list
♦ Audit offshore facility
♦ Finalize contract

Alternately, you may choose to establish your own facility or acquire an existing facility.

3. Implement Phase One

♦ Form teams (local and overseas)
♦ Set up infrastructure
♦ Transfer knowledge (product and process)
♦ Establish knowledge retention mechanisms
♦ Establish a distributed management structure
♦ Establish communication mechanisms and frequencies
♦ Deliver

4. Evaluate results

5. Identify and implement improvements

6. Scale up

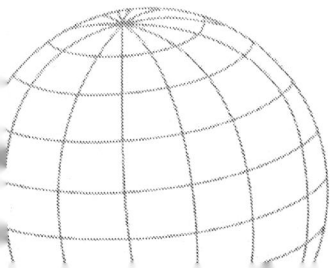

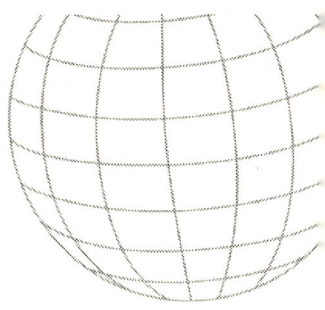

The Author

M. M. "Sath" Sathyanarayan is President of Global Development Consulting Inc. (http://www.GDCInc.biz), an offshore advisory and management services firm. GDC assists companies in going offshore for the first time and to improve existing offshore operations.

Sath is a leading authority on offshoring. His long time experience includes 14 years in offshoring — initially as a Fortune 500 corporation executive leading offshoring, then as startup CEO utilizing offshore resources, now as author and consultant in offshoring. In addition to his roles in offshoring, he provided leadership to product development, support and IT organizations.

Prior to GDC, he held executive and management positions at HP/Tandem Computers – an organization with $2 billion in revenues — where, he pioneered the concept of leveraging offshore resources for strategic advantage. He established and led a worldwide organization of development and technical support personnel working on mission critical applications. This organization improved the cost structure, time-to-market and earnings per share. This initiative succeeded despite many challenges; processes and organization developed under his leadership are still successfully at work after more than 10 years and two acquisitions. Subsequent to HP/Tandem, he was founder and CEO of 24 by 7 Corporation, a professional services firm, which leveraged offshore resources.

Today, Sath is called upon to consult to high-tech companies on offshoring. His clients include Hyperion/Brio Software and Agile Software. In addition to this book, he has published several articles on offshoring and is frequently invited to speak on offshoring at professional organizations.

Sath is a graduate of Virginia Polytechnic and State University. He holds M.S. in Engineering and MBA degrees.

You may contact Sath at:

Global Development Consulting, Inc.
19925 Stevens Creek Blvd.,
Cupertino, CA 94014
(408) 865-0474
info@GDCInc.biz
http://www.GDCInc.biz

Staying Current

Periodically, we send out e-mail alerts and updates on major developments and other time critical information that will enable you to stay current in this fast moving field. To receive, this information, please register at the knowledge center on our web site http://www.GDCinc.biz.

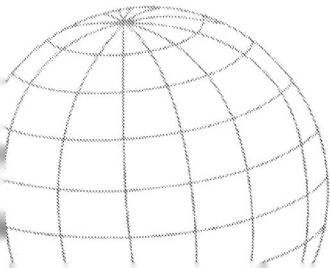

Printed in the United States
22779LVS00003B/376-414